COLLEGE LEADERSHIP FOR COMMUNITY RENEWAL

*Beyond
Community-Based
Education*

James F. Gollattscheck
Ervin L. Harlacher
Eleanor Roberts
Benjamin R. Wygal

COLLEGE
LEADERSHIP
FOR
COMMUNITY
RENEWAL

Jossey-Bass Publishers

San Francisco • Washington • London • 1976

COLLEGE LEADERSHIP FOR COMMUNITY RENEWAL
Beyond Community-Based Education
  by James F. Gollattscheck, Ervin L. Harlacher, Eleanor
  Roberts, and Benjamin R. Wygal

Copyright © 1976 by: Jossey-Bass, Inc., Publishers
       615 Montgomery Street
       San Francisco, California 94111
          &
       Jossey-Bass Limited
       44 Hatton Garden
       London EC1N 8ER

Library of Congress Catalogue Card Number LC 76-19497

International Standard Book Number ISBN 0-87589-299-X

Manufactured in the United States of America

JACKET DESIGN BY WILLI BAUM

FIRST EDITION

Code 7620

The Jossey-Bass Series
in Higher Education

Preface

The term *community renewal college* was first used by one of the authors in a speech at the University of Chicago in 1970. This book grew out of a conviction, shared by all four authors, that few colleges have reexamined their missions in view of current social problems or altered their instructional strategies in view of all that we now know about individual differences in styles of learning and about the need to reach nontraditional students. Changes have been superficial at best. The majority of America's two- and four-year colleges are continuing to operate as though nothing had happened, seemingly oblivious to the many new developments in the various disciplines surrounding education and in education itself—apparently unaware that leaders in other fields are forecasting doom for our communities, and indeed for our society in its present form.

Certainly the curriculum has been updated by sociopolitical events and by obvious technological developments. And a number of colleges were jolted out of their complacency by the student activism of the 1960s. Many of these, however, resumed their repose in the 1970s, when student activism diminished. The current decline in enrollments and prediction of an even greater decline, coupled with the economic slump that has reduced funding, have aroused many colleges and caused many more to begin to question their inaction. Yet even in the late 1970s, we cannot say that colleges, in general, have responded to the changing needs of their constituents or assimilated the ideas advanced by leaders in education and related fields.

We agree with Raymer F. Maguire, Jr., that when the history of American higher education is analyzed, the three most important events will be the Land Grant Colleges Act of 1862 (Morrill Act), the GI Bill, and the development of the comprehensive community college. Each at the time of its development was a significant step forward, but that time has past. The Land Grant Colleges Act broke classical European concepts and traditions of higher education, and made a college education more useful and more easily available to the populace. In time, however, land-grant colleges became major universities almost as prestigious and tradition-bound as the older universities from which they had sprung. By emulating their predecessors in academic excellence and admission standards, they necessarily became more restrictive. The GI Bill made a college education possible for a larger mass of citizens than ever before. But the bill was a student-financial-aid measure, not an educational movement. It brought about no changes in education other than those caused by the sheer number of mature students descending on colleges. The development of the comprehensive community college has had a twofold impact: it has brought postsecondary education within financial and geographic reach of an even larger number of students, and it has brought about important educational changes. The open-door policy of most community colleges, combined with the emphasis on occupational programs and community services, has added a radically new dimension to American postsecondary education. Unfortunately, true commitment to community services and provision for changes in educational programs to compensate for the open door are found more frequently in college catalogs and mission statements than in practice.

We believe that the time has come for a fourth major development in American postsecondary education: the creation of the community renewal college. The deterioration of our communities, the increasing inability of individuals to cope with rapid change, the obsolescence of individuals and social organizations, and the increasing number of citizens with educational needs who are beyond the purview of existing colleges demand a new kind of postsecondary institution. This new college must be committed to the improvement of all aspects of community life.

In this book we attempt to describe a college of the future. It is almost certain that no college at present has become a true community renewal college in every respect, yet all over our nation communities and colleges are beginning to realize they must cooperate if our society is to survive. Many community renewal activities are already being practiced by various colleges and universities. We have included a number of examples and have chosen community renewal activities at seven colleges for presentation in more detail, as case studies. These seven case studies are not isolated examples; many colleges and activities could have been cited. The point is that the practices described in this book are within the present capabilities of America's two- and four-year colleges.

Because the book is both future-oriented and grounded in examples of current practice, it will be of help and of interest, we believe, to all persons concerned with higher education. College policy makers should find much that is challenging on the question of institutional goals. College administrators and future administrators will find practical examples and guidelines for future development. In the educational philosophy and methodology we advocate, scholars of higher education should find much with which to agree, disagree, or suspend judgment.

We do not use a "cookbook" approach: this book contains no step-by-step instructions for creating a community renewal college. Since such an institution must be developed in a community and fitted to the problems and resources of that community, a uniform set of instructions would be impossible.

We do hope that fellow educators will find the book stimulating and that our attempts to synthesize current thought and prac-

tice into future directions for postsecondary education will help
readers succeed in their efforts to create institutions for ever-changing community needs.

September 1976   James F. Gollattscheck
                                          Orlando, Florida

                                          Ervin L. Harlacher
                                          Kansas City, Missouri

                                          Eleanor Roberts
                                          Kansas City, Missouri

                                          Benjamin R. Wygal
                                          Jacksonville, Florida

Contents

COLLEGE LEADERSHIP FOR COMMUNITY RENEWAL

Beyond Community-Based Education

I

The Mission of the Community Renewal College

$\blacklozenge$

A revolution is underway in the United States—a revolution very different from other revolutions this country has experienced and certainly unlike those that other countries have undergone. It is a quiet revolution: there are no bombs, no guns, no marches, no threats and counterthreats. It is happening in the most surprising places: churches, senior-citizen centers, hospitals, public libraries, government buildings, police stations—hardly the places one expects to find a revolution brewing. The revolutionaries are themselves an unlikely lot: housewives and businessmen, elderly retired people and young activists, liberals and conservatives, the college-educated and the illiterate, the wealthy and the poor, government officials and inmates of prisons. Perhaps

1

most surprising of all, emerging as the command posts of the revolution are many of America's colleges.

Everywhere men and women are beginning to realize that the education they received in the past, regardless of how little or how much, cannot sustain them for long in a time of rapid change. They sense that the world in which they live is no longer the world they have known, that the nation is undergoing deep and ever-accelerating changes, and that even the community or neighborhood in which they live no longer offers the comfort of continuity. They recognize that unless they take preventive action, they will become as obsolete as last year's headlines. They are discovering that if they wish to remain in touch with the reality of an ever-changing, ever-new present, they must change themselves—that the only way to survive in a world where so much is new every day is to develop a process for continual self-renewal. They are demanding opportunities for renewal, and leadership to show them the way.

An expanding and ever-accelerating technology renders the training of professional people obsolete in a few years, creates environmental crises that threaten our very existence, and makes it difficult for us to cope with a "world of tomorrow" that somehow seems to have arrived yesterday.

The desire of women to enter the mainstream of American life as full partners is placing demands upon employers, educational institutions, and women themselves, many of whom recognize that they have been ill prepared to compete for jobs and status.

Growing numbers of culturally and economically disadvantaged people, caught in the two related traps of poverty and ignorance, are becoming increasingly impatient in their desire to share in the American "good life."

The plight of older people, no longer content to sit in rocking chairs during their declining years, grows more critical as their ranks swell in number, augmented by earlier and earlier retirement.

This problem of obsolescence and inability to cope with change is not simply a problem of individuals. As people become obsolete and ineffective, entire communities become obsolete, and states and regions weaken. The spreading decline and death of our inner cities and the downtown areas of smaller communities, and the resulting increase in slums and ghettos, are fostering a suburb-versus-city antagonism that grows more volatile daily. Many of the major problems facing our communities and our nation are related to the collective inability of individuals to participate as effective citizens in our changing society. Unfortunately, as social structures weaken and become obsolete, they are less and less able to provide the services that might improve the ability of individuals to improve the community; thus a self-perpetuating cycle of social and individual disability becomes endemic.

The problems of our cities and communities, and of the people who inhabit them, are increasingly difficult to ignore. Time is rapidly running out for ameliorating them. As educators have realized these facts and witnessed the need for continual education and individual and community improvement, they have begun to experiment with several approaches to renewal. Their experiments hold the promise of someday having a profound effect on the nation's entire system of education, but so far those experiments have not ensured that our institutions of higher education will meet the educational needs of these revolutionary times.

First on the scene have been colleges and universities, with an expressed commitment to rural and urban extension services and to continuing education. But far too often, the expansion of their extension services has meant merely the extension of conventional courses and programs to larger numbers of students. As Strother (1972) has pointed out, "Universities have changed remarkably little since Thomas Aquinas lectured at the University of Paris in the middle of the thirteenth century . . . Expansion both of literacy and of the knowledge base have been reflected in the proliferation of courses and in numbers enrolled" (pp. 10–13). And as one faculty member at a leading state university observes about its new "extended university" program, the institution "is marching forward boldly into the 1920s" (Houle, 1973, p. 109).

More recent developments have been the evolution of the "community education" movement, based on the premise that community schools can serve as a central resource to assist in solving community problems, and the emergence of community services as a major function of the community college. Yet, until recently, most educational institutions—including community colleges and community-oriented universities—did little more than provide those services for the community that their educators had decided the community needed. Even today, few institutions are actively engaged in developing community services to their fullest potential. Except for some spotty programs, they remain largely institutions *in* but not *of* their communities. Too many of them assign the director of community services the responsibility of providing merely cultural and recreational diversions (which could be, and frequently are, provided equally well by other community agencies), together with a few educational experiences encapsulated as pleasant placebos and designed primarily for citizens who already are well educated. A surprising number of educators still fail to understand and appreciate why community services viewed as well-conceived, carefully developed learning experiences, rather than as haphazard, ephemeral, or one-shot offerings, are a necessary part of their colleges' operations. Their failure has contributed significantly to the failure of the community-education movement and the community-services function to achieve full acceptance.

Still more recently, under the banner of "community-based education," educators have begun to believe that one of the chief functions of the community-oriented college is to act as a catalyst for bringing community recources as well as college resources to bear on community problems. For example, following the adoption of a plan for greater community-based and performance-oriented education by the Board of Directors of the American Association of Community and Junior Colleges (AACJC) in 1973, many college leaders are beginning to realize that if they are to effect real change in people and communities, a new and different relationship between their institution and the community must develop. With support from the Charles Stewart Mott Foundation, AACJC has expanded upon its original Community Services Project to link together, through a Center for Community Education, more than 900 community and junior colleges, 52 centers for community education in colleges and universities, and 20 centers for community education in state and county offices of education.

Many of these centers are trying to provide for all the educational needs of all community members. They are using advisory councils and community-needs-assessment surveys as vehicles for encouraging community involvement in curriculum planning. But although community colleges probably offer the best hope for community renewal among all institutions of higher education, most of their emphasis on community-based education remains little more than rhetoric. In far too many instances, they are still more "junior" than "community" colleges. They focus their curricular plans on certain predefined student groups—groups that by no means include all community members.

In their defense, it must be pointed out that the course they choose to follow is dictated in large part by the precedent set by society itself. Chancellor Ernest Boyer of the State University of New York (1974, p. 5) explains it this way: "Historically, the span of human life has been chopped up into slices like a great salami, with each section having a special flavor all its own. First, there was the thin slice of early childhood—the time of happy play. Then came a thicker slice—twelve to twenty years, perhaps—devoted almost exclusively to full-time learning. Next, we had the still thicker chunk of full-time work. And finally, came retirement—the little nubbin at the end—characterized by some as 'dignified decline.' " Boyer notes that because institutional patterns have conformed to this long tradition, colleges and universities have ended up catering just to people in one thin slice of the life span, the ages from eighteen to twenty-two—students who were expected to complete their college education before entering the world of work, never to return. Now, abruptly, these patterns are crumbling: not only is there a sudden surge of adult interest in continued learning, but the pool of students of traditional college age is drying up. While employers needing workers with special skills are frequently unable to find them, too many institutions of higher education continue to focus their attention on dwindling numbers of high-school graduates.

The problem, as we can now see, is that these current approaches are inadequate within a time of great human reassessment and change. So far, colleges have cast themselves as "givers"—benevolent institutions in the community that will help the community solve its problems. But they have remained essentially campus-based, faculty-oriented institutions. The community might ask for their help in problem solving—although it seldom does—and the colleges have periodically gone through the obvious exercises of investigating the probable employment needs of business and industry, the kinds of noncredit short courses their faculties might be interested in offering, and the quality of the preparation that their programs give students for further study or entry-level employment. But by relying on the old academic mystique which says that all one has to do in order to be is profess that one is, even so-called community colleges have had only limited success as community institutions. So far, the community-oriented college has simply been *in* the community, holding up its wares for public auction and identifying as its students only small segments of the total community—primarily recent high-school graduates requiring financial and geographical access to low-cost further education.

We have talked a great deal about taking the college to the community. Seldom have we commented on the advantages of *merging* the community with the college, except for proposals of sharing facilities. Merely offering courses in convenient locations throughout the community does not constitute community-based education. Leaving untouched those reservoirs of learners beyond traditional community-college students is far from community service. Despite major efforts to make postsecondary education accessible to all, current delivery systems have not guaranteed that everyone needing further education can take advantage of it. As a result, most colleges have not yet been able to escape their dual historical patterns of class-based tracking and educational inflation—that process by which the educational system expands without narrowing the differences between groups in society and without lowering the barriers to opportunity. The result has been a partly instructed society—not a total learning society.

The time has come to look beyond the conception of extension service, community schools, community service, and community-based education which has presumed their goal to be responsiveness to the learner and the community. What is needed now is a goal that includes not just responsiveness to needs but leadership in the improvement of all aspects of community life. Beyond being community-based, our colleges must now aim at human and community renewal.

A college for community renewal, whether it be a community college, a four-year college, or a university, must be linked to the community in such a manner that it determines its direction and develops its goals through college-community interaction, uses the total community as a learning laboratory and resource, serves as a catalyst to create in the community a desire for renewal, provides a vehicle through which the community educates itself, and evaluates its successes by citizen successes that are recognized as significant by the community itself.

A college for community renewal must no longer be just an agency to provide services to the community; it must be a vital participant in the total renewal process of the community. Such a college will be committed not just to degrees and credentials, not just to job training, and not just to service for the community. It will, rather, be committed to the continual improvement of all aspects of community life and dedicated to the continual growth and development of its citizens and its social institutions. It will assume responsibility for helping to create the revolution in educational expectations as well as ensuring the success of this cause.

In pragmatic terms, the community renewal college delivers the kinds of education community members want and need, not what pedagogues think is good for them. It does so at locations where the learners are, not where conventional college organization indicates they should be. It is guided by open community participation in defining comprehensive learning needs, suggesting solutions, and facilitating delivery, not by the decisions of professional educators and governing boards alone. As it is now emerging, the community renewal college is both learner- and community-oriented. It is no longer merely a "giver" to those who are inclined to accept its gifts; instead, its role is that of cooperator with the community in joint efforts to put people back together in meaningful human endeavors. It is a college that takes an active role in the renewal of its constituents. It constantly avails itself of opportunities to participate in the continual renewal of individuals and thus in the continual restructuring of the community as a whole. It is a true "people's college," not confined to the campus but decentralized and flourishing in the real world of the total community. Its mission is to help people grow in a variety of ways—from finding maximum employment to acquiring the skills necessary for renewal of their neighborhoods and the attitudes for the creation, at last, of a learning society. Touching every citizen, it rejuvenates community pride and serves as an agent of change for the betterment of life at the local level. It lifts the educational achievement of all its constituents. It emphasizes human and community renewal as the cornerstone of every curriculum.

Such a concept of educational institutions sensitive to the survival needs of societies in rapid transition is not entirely new. In 1959, for instance, Mead (p. 5) observed:

When we look realistically at today's world and become aware of what the actual problems of learning are, our conception of education changes radically. Although the educational system remains basically unchanged, we are no longer dealing primarily with the *vertical* transmission of the tried and true by the old, mature, and experienced teacher to the young, immature, and inexperienced pupil in the classroom . . . What is needed and what we are already moving toward is the inclusion of another whole dimension of learning: the lateral transmission to every sentient member of society, of what have just been discovered, invented, created, manufactured, or marketed . . . Is not the break between past and present—and so the whole problem of outdating in our educational system—related to a change in the rate of change? For change has become so rapid that adjustment cannot be left to the next generation. Adults must—not once, but continually—take in, adjust to, use, and make innovations in a steady stream of discovery and new conditions . . . What we call the lateral transmission of knowledge . . . is not an outpouring of knowledge from the "wise old teacher" into the minds of young pupils, as in vertical transmission: Rather it is a sharing of knowledge by the informed with the uninformed, whatever their ages. The primary requisite for the learner is the desire to know.

Mead's concepts of vertical and lateral transmission of knowledge underlie the concept of the community renewal college. The "desire to know" has too often been aborted within the academic structure of the conventional community-based college because of its reliance solely on vertical transmission of knowledge by the "wise old teacher"—and the resulting frustration to the learner and loss to the society.

In "a steady stream of discovery and new conditions," the community renewal college anticipates closer liaison with the community at large and the development of programs and delivery systems to meet its needs. The community renewal college offers community-based curricula, with or without degree requirements so long as the student learns what he needs and wants to know. It aims to break the lock step by offering delivery systems completely divorced from the traditional ones. Whether or not it boasts a formal campus, it operates a network of learning sites throughout the community that provide both formal and informal learning experiences. It utilizes a faculty not solely of academically credentialed persons but also of persons in the community who have demonstrated expertise in their fields of endeavor, thus making the entire community a laboratory for learning.

Recognizing that an increasingly diverse population of learners requires more attention to individual differences and that what is learned is more important than what is taught—that is, valuing learner-centered experiences over teacher-centered experiences—the community renewal college allows the learner to begin where he is, where his previous learning stopped, progress at his own pace according to his individually prescribed learning plan, and achieve competencies that are meaningful to him. People from all walks of life and many age groups are enabled to take advantage of almost unlimited learning opportunities that fulfill individual needs and desires through a new and unique type of education. In an introduction to a film on individualized instruction, K. Patricia Cross stated: "The dramatic impact of open admissions on the establishment of higher education has been the flood of diverse kinds of students into colleges. Their needs differ in many ways from the students that higher education has been used to serving in the past. We are finding that providing learning programs for an increasingly diverse population of learners requires more attention to individual differences. I consider the individualization of instruction of such import to higher education throughout the rest of this century that I have termed these years the beginning of the instructional revolution" (*Fulfilling the Promise of the Open Door*).

The community renewal college is designed to facilitate the exercise of every citizen's right to education beyond whatever level he attained in previous schooling, whether or not he seeks to qualify for a degree.

Since degrees and credentials represent extended periods of

formal instruction, society has come to regard them as evidence of "better" education; often they merely signify the fallacy that the education a student receives between high-school graduation and entry into his life's work is sufficient to carry him through a lifetime. Perhaps this was true at an earlier time in the nation's history, when knowledge was relatively stable. But in the last quarter of the twentieth century, when knowledge gained during a college career is becoming obsolete almost before the ink on the graduate's diploma is dry, it is wholly erroneous. "At some point," say Hesburgh and his associates (1973, p. x), "there has to be a realization that the aim of all this education is learning and knowledge, not the degrees gained."

Conventional colleges have done nothing, or at most very little, thus far to change society's credential-oriented attitude. They have talked a great deal about developing the individual student to his fullest potential, but this has usually meant his ability to achieve degrees. Such concern for degrees is in direct conflict with national and local needs assessments, which indicate that through 1980, four jobs out of five will require more than a high-school education but less than a four-year-college degree.

With no intention to denigrate the value of a degree, we should point out that not every student in need of further education has the time and the financial resources to devote the prescribed two years of formal instruction to acquiring one. The community renewal college takes a larger view of the education process, providing besides formalized learning experiences those of an informal nature that contribute to the individual's acquisition or expansion of competencies and his productive use of what he has learned. The community renewal college is dedicated to the proposition that human renewal—the upgrading of every citizen in its community—is its primary and overriding purpose. Accordingly, two strong planks in its philosophic platform are that society is only as great as the individuals who compose it, and that, like democracy, society is not an heirloom to be handed down from one generation to another. Rather, because the conditions of its environment are perennially in flux, society must be re-created by generation after generation so that the costly decay of communities and the wasteful erosion of human resources can be prevented. This truth implies the need to reject the concept that an individual's ability to accumulate credits is the ultimate measure of his worth, the need to help every member of the community acquire the basic skills and knowledge necessary for effective functioning in a world increasingly fraught with crises, the need to inculcate students with the understanding and belief that education is continual throughout life, and the need to stimulate the intellectual curiosity that makes them eager to learn as their experience of life reveals areas of ignorance.

Discarding the notion that certain dates, names, formulas, literary works, and atomic weights belong in everyone's intellectual kit, along with the notion that credentialism is the single criterion for admission of students, the community renewal college provides a center for postsecondary education with emphasis on learner goals rather than institutional goals. Its aim is to offer educational experiences beyond what citizens usually achieve. As a nontraditional institution, it can operate on a formal campus or on no campus at all. It can provide college credit or no credit at all. And because its primary concern is for the learner himself, it emphasizes multimedia, multimodal, self-instructional learning systems and continuous-progress (freely scheduled) courses.

The community renewal college stresses the student's determination of his own goals, identification of how he proposes to reach those goals, and methods of evaluating how well he is progressing. It also provides for flexible supervision by competent teachers and counselors of all his activities that constitute acquiring his education. It allows for flexible grouping and scheduling, independent study, self-paced learning, hands-on (laboratory and internship) experience, and community internships. In short, the overall goal is to teach students how to learn, so that, more than merely fostering the desire for lifelong learning, the community renewal college may give them the insights that lead eventually to self-actualization.

The discussion above has emphasized the nontraditional aspects of the community renewal college—the radical departures from what have long been established as educational patterns at the college level. Experience has shown that a large segment of the community still wants degrees, diplomas, and certificates; therefore, the traditional must also be considered. And because the community renewal college places higher value on the individual than on the institution, it underscores its ability to serve a wide-ranging clientele, regardless of individual learning needs. The community renewal college recognizes its obligation to provide the comprehensive structure for transfer and general education, occupational/technical education, counseling and guidance, and community services—for many students who may properly be categorized as "nontraditional" still covet a degree that signifies a formal college education. Even in these most traditional of programs, the community renewal college is community-based and performance-oriented.

The community renewal college offers a new model of education, one that is committed to the needs of society and dedicated to renewal in all its forms: human renewal for all our people; urban renewal of our cities and neighborhoods; environmental renewal of the greater communities we serve; political renewal, so critical in a republic based on the concept of rule by the people; and even, perhaps, the moral and spiritual renewal of a great nation.

Renewal implies more than the mere offering of services to the community. Contemporary society is replete with examples of "servicing human beings to death while never answering their deepest needs," thus guaranteeing a future of frustration, despair, and alienation for the people of our communities. Renewal also implies more than mere penetration into the community. It implies a new style of community action to replace the service-oriented systems of delivery to which so many human beings have become addicted. Renewal is a process of regeneration, of restoring life where there is death, whether it be for the individual or for the community. Renewal is what the learning process is all about.

Traditionally, the mission of education has been the emancipation of the young. A community renewal college must likewise seek to provide emancipation, not of the young alone but of all the people within its community; emancipation, that is, from the restrictions of ignorance and socioeconomic disadvantage—unemployment, substandard housing, inadequate schooling, poverty, and filth —and emancipation from environmental stagnation and pollution, but not emancipation from the community itself.

It would serve little purpose to belabor the point that the education of adults is the pressing need of the present and will constitute the focus of the future. To meet that need requires an immediate accommodation of postsecondary education to the life-styles of the new students: off-campus classes and activities, nondegree instructional personnel, a movement away from rigid admissions requirements, and a disregard for the academic calendar—all of which challenges tradition. But the community renewal college is not concerned with the preservation of tradition, except for those aspects of it that are adaptable to the new concept for new clientele.

The community renewal college is not a substandard version of the traditional college; it offers different kinds of education for different kinds of students, and maintains high standards that are true to its own purposes. It has been stated that nontraditional education provides what people want—the ability to provide for the necessities of life and for the good life. This proposition, however, is not central to the philosophy of the community renewal college. Important as this pragmatic aspect of learning is, the larger purpose of education is to make people know how to live zestfully, meaningfully—how to think, feel, understand, and, most important, act with intelligence.

The concept of a community renewal college is not mere theory or idealism. Already many American colleges and universities have adopted parts of the idea. Typical of these efforts are the University Without Walls Consortium initiated by the Union for Experimenting Colleges and Universities, the new Coastline Community College of the Coast Community College District in California, and the Peralta College for Non-Traditional Study of the Peralta Community College District in Oakland and Berkeley, California. Several institutions in the planning stage illustrate the concept: the "New Dimensions" of the Los Angeles Community College District, and three community colleges without walls under development as alternative approaches in Pennsylvania. But among the clearest examples is Metropolitan State University in Minnesota.

CASE STUDY: METROPOLITAN STATE UNIVERSITY

Metropolitan State University (formerly Minnesota Metropolitan State College), in Minneapolis and Saint Paul, Minnesota, was created by the Minnesota state legislature in June 1971. It is a member of the state university system, which includes six other universities throughout the state, and it is the only state university in the Twin Cities, the major metropolitan area in Minnesota.

Metro U received its initial funding from the legislature in 1971 to plan and operate during the 1971–1973 biennium; it enrolled its first fifty students in February 1972. By 1976 it had grown to the point of having eight hundred graduates and an enrollment of sixteen hundred students. The average age of its students is thirty-four; about 46 percent are women and 8 percent are racial minorities, which is almost twice the percentage of minorities in the metropolitan area population. Tuition varies among students and averages $500 per calendar year. Metro U operates year-round out of centers in the downtown areas of Minneapolis and Saint Paul. It received its full accreditation from the North Central Association of Colleges and Secondary Schools in July 1975.

Metropolitan State University has several distinctive characteristics: it is designed to serve adults and other underserved populations in the metropolitan area; it operates without a campus; it is a competency-based, community-based, upper-division institution; it awards a degree (it offers a B.A. only) for learning accomplished in a self-designed program; and it emphasizes the lifelong learning of its graduates. These aspects of the Metro U program are set forth in its five basic educational tenets, which determine the university's nature and focus.

The first tenet, perhaps the most unusual, states: "The University vests in each individual student responsibility for and authority over his or her education. The university vests in its officers and faculty responsibility for and authority over teaching and for determining whether or not a student has given adequate evidence that he or she has achieved his or her educational objectives." This confidence in the ability of adults to make mature, responsible decisions about their education, with the advice and counsel of the faculty and staff of the university, permeates the institution. Degree programs are individually designed by the students to meet their personal needs and to take into account their individual characteristics as citizens, learners, and workers. The procedures and policies of the institution are designed to support this basic tenet and to promote the individualized nature of student programs. At the same time, these policies and procedures are designed to allow maximum input from the university and its staff in each student's development of the individualized degree plan.

The second tenet of the institution relates to Metro U's commitment to competency-based education. It states: "The university records a student's educational progress in terms of the competence the student achieves and *not* in terms of the number of courses or other units of experience which the student undertakes to achieve competences." *Competence* is defined as what an individual knows or knows how to do in a particular subject area at a specified level; a subject area must have both a theoretical and a practical base. The level of each competence is judged against some norm, the student's personal goal, the domain of the subject area, or a rating scale of some kind. (A competency statement might read: "Knows the principles and techniques of analyzing society for the values, customs and mores of its subgroups and can apply that knowledge in analyzing the Native American subgroup as it exists in the Twin Cities.") The institutional focus is on learning outcomes, whether the learning took place prior to enrollment at Metro U or in some learning opportunity that Metro U sponsored. A common saying at Metro is that "it does not matter where you learned it, why you learned it, from whom you learned it, or how you learned it; the question is whether you know it."

To assist students in achieving competences, the university sponsors group learning opportunities (courses), internships, independent studies, and other learning opportunities through a variety of community resources. Less than half of the learning represented on student transcripts is through Metro U–sponsored courses. Many competences which students acquire are unique and personal, such as those gained through a joint program with a local arts organization which provided a "poet in residence" to Metro U students and to the community. A major focus of the Learning Resources Office is to provide students with a wide variety of learning opportunities in the community, through other activities than those that are university-sponsored. All such learning activities are designed to help students acquire competences in as many ways and in as many areas as possible.

This second tenet also supports another aspect of Metro U— the narrative transcript. The narrative transcript sets forth the competences that a student possesses, how the competences were achieved, how they were evaluated, who evaluated them, and a brief, narrative evaluative statement by the evaluator.

The third tenet of the university states: "The university believes that whenever appropriate, students should be encouraged to make use of community resources, including human resources and events controlled by agencies and organizations external to the university, to achieve their educational goals."

One aspect of this commitment is that the university has no campus—it utilizes the facilities of churches, schools, private agencies, governmental agencies, and the like. This tenet is also the basis for the community faculty and its role in the Metro U teaching/learning process. Metro U has a small core of twenty-five permanent faculty members who serve as advisers, planners, and facilitators, but most teaching is done by the three hundred community faculty members, qualified professionals in the community who teach in the areas in which they work. For example, the personnel manager of a multinational corporation headquartered in the Twin Cities teaches personnel management; an accountant with a major national accounting firm teaches several different accounting courses. Finally, Metro U students are encouraged to achieve their goals through the use of learning opportunities sponsored by other educational institutions and learning resources in the area.

These area opportunities are quite varied and can be made use of in a number of ways, such as participating in courses through institutions such as the Gestalt Center, the Adlerian Institute, the American Banking Association and the Small Business Administration. Metro U also recently co-sponsored with a local conference center a seminar on budget and management in art organizations for Metro U students and key personnel in local art organizations. In addition, Metro U has initiated a learning resource information and reference system known as the MILL (Metropolitan Information and Learning Library) to assist students and interested personnel in finding learning resources in the community. It is designed to collect and disseminate—either in person or by telephone—information about potential teachers, classes, seminars, workshops, books, and other learning resources. Further, an agreement with a local reference library, coupled with an inter-library exchange system

(MINITEX), provides students with access to the resources of nearly every library in the state.

The fourth tenet at Metro U provides the students with guidance as to the meaning of a baccalaureate degree. "The university recommends that each student receiving a degree demonstrate a high level of competence in each of these areas of life: communications and basic learning; the responsibilities of being a member of a self-governing community; work; recreation; and personal development and social awareness. To achieve competence in the areas listed means that students must know and employ many of the arts, sciences, humanities, and applied disciplines. It also frequently means that students will require types of knowledge and understanding which vary significantly from the types usually associated with higher education, particularly experientially-based knowledge and affective knowledge; the university respects the broadening of the concept of what it means to be learned which is thereby implied." This tenet expresses Metro's approach to education, and it is one of the primary elements stressed as students prepare their degree plans. An early study indicated that approximately one half of the competences required on students' transcripts were in vocational areas, but that percentage is declining. This tenet contains the commitment of Metro U to the role of the student as an urban citizen, since every student is expected to demonstrate competence in each of the five competence areas.

The fifth tenet provides: "The university expects that those upon whom it confers degrees will be life-long, self-directed learners committed to excellence in their learning." The basis for this tenet —that living and learning are inextricably tied together—results in Metro's commitment to teaching its students how to learn.

The educational process at Metro U is designed to implement these tenets. Students, having satisfied the 90 quarter credit entrance requirements (whether by earning actual course credits or by demonstrating that they have achieved the equivalent through life-experience learning), must attend and complete the course Individualized Educational Planning. During this course the students develop their degree plans with the guidance and assistance of a detailed text and significant faculty involvement. A student entering with the minimum entrance requirements must include twenty-four competences in the degree plan. At completion of the Individualized Educational Planning course, when the student has developed a degree plan and has had it approved, he or she becomes a degree candidate and is assigned an adviser. With the adviser's help, the student proceeds to implement the degree plan and submits evidence to the university after attaining each competence in the plan. The assessment office, staffed by faculty, determines whether the student has submitted adequate evidence of the competence, and certifies competences to the registrar for inclusion on the student's narrative transcript. Graduations are held three times each year, on the average, in various community facilities.

Metro U was initiated in 1971 as a self-conscious experiment in student-designed, competency-based, community-based higher education for previously underserved populations. In keeping with its initial purpose, it has continually modified and improved its processes and policies in order to better serve its students. In carrying out these ends, it has received local, regional, national, and international recognition as a model alternative approach to higher education.

As Metropolitan State University illustrates, there is a difference between *offering* to the community the educational experiences educators think citizens should have and *delivering* the experiences and competencies they actually need and want. This is the difference between a traditional institution and a community renewal college.

With examples such as Metro U and new community colleges without walls, the suggestion in 1974 by Alan Pifer, president of the Carnegie Corporation of New York, now seems more feasible than even he thought it might be: "Community colleges should start thinking about themselves from now on only secondarily as a sector of higher education and regard as their primary role community leadership." Addressing the American Association of Community and Junior Colleges, he cast the community college in a key leadership role for the reconstruction of American society. "Other institutions have a part to play, of course, but I see the community college as the essential leadership agency . . . They can become the hub of a network of institutions and community agencies—the higher schools, industry, the church, voluntary agencies, youth groups, even the prison system and the courts—utilizing their educational resources and, in turn, becoming a resource for them" (Gleazer, 1974b, p. 7).

So far, the community-based college's error in taking this leadership role—if, indeed, it has been an error—lies in the fact that it has overemphasized its role as catalyst in initiating that vague something called "community action" and "social change." Now the community-based college and the community-based-education movement need to reevaluate themselves in view of their focus as facilitators of the American dream of universal participation in effective citizenship, involvement in satisfying and productive work, and sharing in the benefits of our social and cultural opportunities. Gass (1974, p. 23) recently wrote:

> There is everywhere a demand for a more human pattern of economic growth that takes into account the satisfactions, as well as goods and services, that individuals seek as part of affluence.
>
> Education should be the pioneer of this move toward a more individualized society. When all the ink has dried on the objectives of education, it will surely be recognized that the unique role of education is to be the bridge between the individual and society. It socializes individuals and also promotes the understanding that is the seed of change and even revolt. Education places the individual in the social structure, yet it remains the liberator from the existing class structure.

A community tends to decline and to be in need of renewal as individual obsolescence grows. Beyond community service, beyond community education, beyond the community-based college, the community renewal college gets close to the real roots of obsolescence—the individuals who compose the community—by concentrating on the *human*-renewal aspects of its offerings.

II

Learning About the
Clientele for Renewal

Unlike its predecessor, the conventional college, the community renewal college is much more than a college in a community, offering its traditional programs to those who want them. The community renewal college actively seeks to serve the needs of the growing number of what would at one time have been called "nontraditional" students: those who cannot afford the time or cost of conventional further education; those whose interests and talents are not served by traditional education; those who have been displaced by automation and who must retool themselves in midcareer; those whose previous educational experiences have precluded their acquiring the necessary skills to move into the higher echelons of learning; those whose educational progress has been interrupted by illness, military service, or other temporary conditions beyond their control; those who are elderly and have come passively to accept the questionable blessings of retirement; and the multitudes caught up in the lock step of tradition, believing mistakenly that college is four walls, semester-length courses, earning a degree, only for the culturally and intellectually elite, and, most significant of all, beyond their reach.

These categories of learners are only exemplary; there are many more. If the services the community renewal college proposes are to be truly effective, it must find the means to reach all such groups. Where to find them can be determined only by a community analysis. Although we probably pass many possible students on the street every day of our lives, we may not recognize them as such because they are nontraditional—neither high school graduates nor perennial students. They have already demonstrated their reluctance to come to the college; therefore, the college must go to them.

Doomsday forecasts of declining college enrollments are based on the traditional delivery system of higher education developed in the late nineteenth and early twentieth centuries and basically unchanged since. This system assumed that a college or university required a physical location where students and teachers met, and that a college education consisted of four years of courses. Expanded access will result in a larger market and a new breed of student, thus exploding the experts' predictions of declining enrollments. According to Gleazer (1974b, p. 8),

Within current confines alone, we know that if every "housewife" took one "course" every other year, the impact would be an instant tripling of 1972 enrollments. Outside those confines it is mind boggling to think of the market represented by the "learning force" at large:

Item: The postwar babies now 26 years old will be available for postsecondary education through the year 2000.

Item: In only 26 years half the population will be 50 years of age or older.

Item: A recent survey by the Ontario Institute for Studies in Education indicated that most adults spend about 700 hours a year at anywhere from one to half a dozen "learning projects" outside higher education.

Item: Approximately 11.2 million adults (ages 18–60) exclusive of full-time students are now engaged in learning experiences sponsored by noneducational institutions
such as labor unions, private industry, museums, professional trade associations, and governmental agencies.
A number larger than all students now enrolled in
colleges and universities.
Zero education growth? Hardly.

In the past, expanded access to higher education has meant
allowing greater numbers of persons in the 18–24 age group to attend college. In the future, according to a February, 1973, report
of The Joint Committee on the California Master Plan for Higher
Education (The Community Services Catalyst, 1974, p. 45),
"postsecondary education will be less campus-bound and will serve
persons in all age groups. Many individuals have neither the time
nor resources to attend a conventional college or university. Yet,
their needs for postsecondary education are often at least as great as
the needs of those people who attend conventional colleges and universities." In consequence, the community renewal college must
have as its foundation basic items of information about the community that will constitute its clientele. The mortar that binds together
these diverse building blocks of information is a unique blend of
patience, perseverance, and cooperative sharing and searching with
the community. A new look toward the community will require a
new view, with the community, of community needs as they relate
both to existing college programs and to potential human and educational services.

A needs assessment is only a part of the community analysis
needed by the community renewal college. Knowledge of a community's needs is of utmost importance if the college is to serve the
community effectively, but a total community analysis will reveal
strengths and resources in the community as well as needs. A knowledge of these will enable the college to build upon existing community resources, to serve as a clearinghouse for matching discovered needs with existing resources, and to extend its potential as
a change agent by working through existing organizations and agencies in the community.

Moreover, whereas a thorough analysis may be undertaken only at long intervals, the need for up-to-date information about the community is continuous. The community renewal college must develop systems that allow for a free flow of needed information about the community on a regular basis. The college must make spot checks of various constituencies, monitor certain community data, and use its established links to the community for two-way communication at all times. Ideally, the community renewal college should know as much about daily and weekly conditions in its community as the weather bureau does about weather conditions in its area. Unfortunately, instruments to gauge the conditions of the community as effective as barometers and thermometers are not available. The college must be innovative in developing its own instruments and systems for continual analysis.

The benefits of such gauging systems will be multifaceted. Existing programs will improve. The community college staff involved will gain new insights into the community as well as an enthusiasm for the community-based approach to community college education. Lines of communication will open and cooperative links will develop between the college and various organizations and agencies. Benefits to the public-relations program will be realized through a better understanding of the constituent community as well as through the general public awareness generated by the several community-study activities. Overall, the services of the community college will change and expand.

To our knowledge, no model exists for a comprehensive community-needs assessment. There are, however, a number of partial approaches. For example, most feasibility studies for the establishment of community colleges or the development of physical facilities center on enrollment projections based on high school data. Employer-needs surveys are generally based on the needs of industry rather than those of people, and, most other needs-assessment activities have been limited to particular target groups and target areas or have concentrated on program concerns. A piecemeal approach to data collection and analysis would include the following phases: an ongoing effort to search out new information, and the development of cooperative relationships with various groups and agencies, can yield a sound basis for decisions concerning the development of community-based programs. Then the information and ideas thus obtained must be combined into integrated proposals, and each need assigned a priority; this task requires effort by the community as well as the college. Continued analysis and evaluation will sharpen assessment abilities as well as validate (or redirect) programing.

On the pages that follow, the various avenues to exploring community needs will be given a general overview, beginning with a basic description of a community.

What Is a Community?

The word *community* may denote a social group of any size whose members reside in the same locality, have a common government, and have a common cultural and historical heritage. The word may also simply indicate the public at large or a group of individuals who possess similar characteristics or hold similar viewpoints or beliefs. As one views a community (in the first sense) one immediately begins to identify groups of people and, subsequently, individuals who form the groups. Each group may be called a "community" because its members have either common beliefs or common practices—or, perhaps, the group holds what is popularly called a "community of interests."

"Community groups" within the larger community come into being in a variety of ways. Some groups form according to "natural selection," such as ethnic groups. Others are self-selecting, either by the group or by the individual. The members of a self-selecting group engage in a common form of employment, recreation, or some other activity, and either the group or the individual has full selective opportunity. Finally, some groups are quasiselective: individuals find themselves unintentionally selected into such groups or unintentionally select themselves. Community groups that form by "natural selection" include socioeconomic groups, ethnic groups, minority groups, and other affinity groups, as well as groups "selected" by age, sex, or physical or mental well-being. Self-selecting groups based on employment include labor unions, the civil service, the armed services, a variety of professional organizations, and even the group of migrant workers. Perhaps welfare groups might also be included in this category. Self-selecting nonwork groups include those related to religion, recreation, volunteerism, or social action. A number of groups, however, fall into a gray area of quasiselection, or unintentional selection. These include people who live within the law or outside the law, those who are imprisoned, those who are addicted to drugs or alcohol, and those who suffer certain kinds of mental disorders.

Some groups consist of people who are, whether by choice or not, in transition. Because this is an age of rapid change, people are constantly adjusting to new geographical settings, jobs, families, and the like. Transitional groups include, for example, the newly divorced, the newly retired, recently discharged veterans, those who are ill or are recuperating, immigrants, tourists, and middle-aged housewives returning to paid employment.

Quantification of information about the people in a community results in valuable baseline data for initial efforts to determine educational needs. Much of that information is readily available.

Gathering Basic Information on a Community

The most easily accessible source of general information on a community is the United States Bureau of the Census, which has a wealth of data concerning residents' personal characteristics, occupations, incomes, and so forth, all of which gives an overall picture of the community.

Personal characteristics listed for a local population are race; age, by sex (there are twenty-three age categories); relationship to head of household; type of family (usual family unit, or children living with other relatives, or grandparent(s) living with family, or other type of family); number of own children; and marital status. Occupational data indicate employment rate, by sex, of residents sixteen years and over; occupations, by sex (some two dozen occupational categories are listed); industries in which workers are employed (fifteen categories are listed here); and, finally, the class of workers to which residents belong: number privately employed, number employed in government, and number self-employed. Income data state income by household (fifteen income ranges are listed); by source (wages and salaries, farming, self-employment, or social security and welfare); by relationship of income to the poverty level; and, for households whose incomes are below the poverty level, by size and composition of household.

A variety of other population items are also included in census data: number of years of schooling completed; weeks worked during the past year; occupational status and place of residence five years ago; their mother tongues; the grade level of school or college, if currently enrolled; vocational training completed; the means of transportation to work; and the presence and duration of any disability. Information related to housing is also detailed: the number of units at the same address; presence of a telephone, a kitchen, a flush toilet, a bathtub or shower; presence of air conditioning; the condition of housing units; and possession of an automobile, a television, a radio, and basic appliances. Although many of these data may appear extraneous to an assessment of a community's educational needs, none should be totally ignored at the initial stage of making the needs assessment.

Besides the Bureau of the Census, many other agencies, governmental and private, regularly report data that are useful in analyzing a community. One basic source of information, for instance, is the state department of employment services. In many states this department monthly and annually compiles information related to job listings at its local offices. Among the data gathered by these offices are the number of openings listed during the period; the number of openings filled during the period; how long each position was open; whether it remained unfilled or was canceled; education and experience required for each listing; and pay range for that job.

Many other social and educational agencies also provide routine reports, usually of a statistical nature. They focus upon such areas as vocational rehabilitation, family services, criminal justice, health services, housing, consumer services, and particular population groups such as the aged, the handicapped, and the poor and disadvantaged. A recent survey of a medium-sized city yielded a list of some 200 such agencies in addition to schools and churches.

Most such agencies also prepare reports of special surveys,

which are easily accessible. One must scan many reports, however, if documents containing pertinent information about the community are to be located, since not all special-survey reports will be applicable. Those prepared by housing and urban-development agencies contain valuable information. Similarly, reports pulled together by the research departments of newspapers and other media, in their pursuit of background information for news stories, are of great interest to the community college. And the United Way, together with its affiliated agencies, sometimes gathers special information about a community that is available from no other source.

A number of communities have an organized community-planning council, which coordinates social-agency surveys and data-collecting activities conducted by separately organized councils or groups. Among these are usually councils on criminal justice, on aging, on family services, on economic opportunity, and the like. In addition, ad hoc groups with a great interest in community action and social renewal frequently produce reports that are extremely valuable in determining educational needs. Many of these groups, in conference, focus on community problems and later issue a report accompanied by recommendations, so that lines of action are already defined. As another source of special reports, the local chamber of commerce is a reservoir of highly useful information.

Studies generated internally by the college itself will likewise yield a wealth of important information on the community, especially as it relates to the college. Basic admissions and student-record data as well as reports required by external agencies are readily available, though sometimes difficult to analyze. In such instances, the office of institutional research will be of immeasurable assistance, because it likely will have summaries and analyses of the reports already prepared as well as pertinent reports of its own studies.

A great resource for information also exists among faculty and students. As a part of their individual professional development, college faculty and staff members may enter into research that can shed light on various aspects of the community; and college students may be required to make surveys as part of a course. Because the individuals composing the college community are also members of the larger community, their rapport with persons and groups in the larger community is likely to be highly productive. Finally, the college's own master plan is a valuable source of local data, especially since it probably has received intensive scrutiny and analysis during its development.

The sources of basic data describing a community which are discussed above do not exhaust the possibilities for discovery in this area. But such sources, when reports from them are brought together, do show what information remains to be gathered in order to complete a community profile.

Gathering Additional Information

Once the college has gathered its baseline data, it should determine what additional studies will be needed to fill in the blank areas and produce a total picture of the community. What are some of the strategies for conducting these additional studies to help analyze a community and its needs? This area will require much research in the near future as colleges attempt to reconstitute themselves as community renewal colleges.

First, a careful analysis and categorization must be made of the various elements of information already obtained, so that missing elements may be identified. Second, procedures should be established for acquiring the new information. Efforts of colleges to complete their analyses of community needs usually take the form of occupational-needs surveys, attitudinal studies of individuals in the community, surveys of persons interested in taking courses, and solicitation of community involvement in goal setting.

Following is a brief description of some of the study techniques used in analyzing certain kinds of community needs.

Occupational Needs Surveys. Although many researchers contend that surveying employers is not a valid means of determining real occupational needs, such surveys are important because they often validate data produced by other research as well as give the "employer community" active involvement in the process of needs assessment. A number of state departments of education and their divisions of vocational/technical education or community college education provide forms for conducting employer surveys. In addition, many nationwide and local consulting and research firms have developed detailed strategies for conducting such surveys. Generally, information regarding employer needs may be acquired quite easily.

Community Awareness and Public Opinion. Individuals' and groups' perceptions of their needs and of the services they require are very important in planning. In fact, individual (and community) awareness of issues and the development of public opinion related to those issues are essential to the fabric of a democratic society. As Abraham Lincoln remarked, "With public opinion on its side, everything succeeds. With public opinion against it, nothing succeeds."

Scientifically conducted public opinion surveys have been useful to government officials in evaluating and improving their services, because such surveys reveal (1) constituents' satisfaction or dissatisfaction with the quality of particular services, (2) facts such as the numbers and characteristics of users and nonusers of various services, (3) the reasons that certain services are disliked or not used, (4) potential demands for new services, and (5) citizens' opinions on various community issues, including their feelings of alienation from government and officials.

It is not always easy, however, for a college to obtain an accurate understanding of how communities feel about a wide range of issues related to educational services. In such instances, use of a community-awareness survey can help to reveal community opinion in a number of pertinent areas. Survey objectives might include assisting the college in the following efforts: (1) improving and expanding its educational programs; (2) gearing its programs to meet educational needs as perceived by members of the community; (3) evaluating the effect of its promotional efforts within the community; (4) facilitating attendance through the removal of barriers to entrance; (5) providing information about the college to the entire community; (6) evaluating the quality of its programs and their impact on the community; (7) planning programs based on potential community demand.

The results of the survey will bear on the college's analysis of its program objectives and the improvement of its programs.

Promotional activities, student development, vocational/technical programs, outreach programs—all can be affected advantageously.

Proposed Model

A model for assessing community needs, particularly those for vocational training and programing, might have as its broad objective (K. D. Tucker, 1974–1975, p. 2) "to . . . allow the educational system to: (a) rank the community's educational needs in their order of importance, (b) develop alternative plans to meet those needs, (c) determine budget allocation guidelines according to needs priorities, (d) monitor the benefit or value of the need as compared to its cost, i.e., discover if fulfilling a need is economically feasible, and (e) develop a continuing dynamic system to evaluate the educational system's effectiveness in meeting community needs."

Because every college today faces the urgent need to provide the most relevant programs possible with its limited resources, the model should specify a consistent, dependable method for identifying the changing patterns in needs of potential students so that workable plans could be implemented.

Consequently, a comprehensive model might well include strategies for the following operations:

1. Develop a data-collecting system to determine the needs of the total population of the community.
2. Establish a hierarchy of community educational needs.
3. Relate the needs to one another according to the geographical distribution of the community population characteristics.
4. Enable the college to measure its present performance against fulfillment of the needs identified by the study.
5. For fulfilling the needs, state measurable, concrete goals, and generate alternative plans (both short- and long-range) for achieving them.
6. Develop cost-utility analysis and apply it to the alternative proposals for achieving the goals.
7. Implement the alternative solutions selected in the cost-utility analysis to meet each objective.
8. Monitor the results of the implemented solutions to evaluate their effectiveness through follow-up analysis.

9. Direct "new money requirements" when priorities are beyond budget constraints.
10. Improve community relations by encouraging greater public understanding of and involvement with the educational system.
11. Improve lines of communication between the community and the total educational system, leading to continuous educational exchange.
12. Increase administrators' awareness of how their educational institution can meet community needs through improved management.

Major social problems and needs (in addition to educational ones) must be identified when surveying the community so that effective delivery systems can be developed. Questions to be answered concerning these problems and needs might include, but not be limited to, the following:

Income/Poverty
1. What is the median income of the community?
2. Where are pockets of poverty, if any, located?
3. What independent community efforts are being made to relieve the plight of the poor? How can these efforts be coordinated with those made by the community renewal college?
4. What percentage of the poor are unemployed or underemployed?
5. What percentage do the poor represent of the population not served by postsecondary education?

Urbanization/Population Growth/Density
1. Has the composition of the population changed during the past five years?
2. Has the population increased or decreased during the past five years?
3. What is the percentage of immigration from rural areas?
4. Are housing accommodations concentrated in urban or suburban areas?
5. To what extent has urban renewal been undertaken by the community?
6. Are low-cost housing units currently available or planned for construction in the immediate future?

7. What are the geographical locations of ethnic concentrations? Are these concentrations single or mixed?
8. If single concentrations exist, have they developed because their residents prefer to live among people with similar ethnic backgrounds?
9. Are ethnic concentrations coextensive with poverty pockets?
10. What is the crime rate in the community?
11. What provisions are made for citizen safety, and how effective are they?

Clientele
1. What is the percentage of one-parent families, with their accompanying problems? Will parents have trouble obtaining babysitting services?
2. What percentage of the population do not have enough to eat each day? Where are they located?
3. What level of educational achievement have potential clients attained? Are they functionally literate?
4. How many potential clients have difficulty understanding instructions presented in English? What can be done to anticipate this problem?
5. Among the population, are there people who have avoided learning English as a second language because of a desire to preserve their cultural heritage?
6. What percentage of students leave high school with learning disabilities or deficiencies?
7. How many persons in the service area have learning disabilities or deficiencies?
8. How can the different learning styles among the target populations be identified?
9. At what level has previous learning stopped for each potential learner?
10. What are the career and personal goals of each potential learner?
11. What is the demographic profile of full-time and part-time students?
12. What percentage of potential clients have physical handicaps? What kinds of handicaps?
13. How many potential learners will require financial assistance? What amount and what kind?

14. What special services and programs will be required to accommodate veterans?

15. What special programs and services must be designed to attract and successfully serve the "new students"?

General Considerations

1. How is the community meeting health-care needs?
2. What social agencies does the community, or private segments of the community, support?
3. How effective is the public educational system (elementary and secondary)?
4. What employment opportunities does the community offer?
5. Is there a transportation system that can accommodate a majority of workers and students?
6. To what extent has the energy crisis produced problems in the community?

The foregoing questions, of course, are by no means exhaustive. Answers to them (as to others less general) are essential if the community renewal college is to develop programs and delivery systems to meet community needs on a far broader scale than is now being done. The college can also rely on sources outside itself to provide necessary information about its host community. Religious organizations, for instance, have used the Delphi technique in a number of situations, including the planning of some community-wide programs, and are usually eager to cooperate with educational institutions in meeting identified community needs. Moreover, the Institutional Goals Inventory, developed by the Educational Testing Service of Princeton, New Jersey, is both easily obtainable and in computerized form. These two techniques have the objective of developing a consensus about goals and assigning priorities to such goals.

Another means of assessing how well a college is doing in serving its community as a community-based, performance-oriented institution is suggested in a study by Yarrington (1975). Yarrington's study, which was field-tested in a community college in the Portland, Oregon, area during the summer of 1975, utilized structured interviews. Fifty-four persons—trustees, administrators, faculty members, students, classified staff members, local citizens, and representatives of nearby colleges—were interviewed over a four-week period using thirty-three questions relating to community-based and performance-oriented education. His definitions of these two concepts are generally compatible with those presented in Chapter One. His definition of performance-oriented education, however, adds the dimension of institutional accountability (p. 10): "The institution has demonstrated commitment and skill in evaluating its responses to identified community needs and reporting findings in terms citizens can easily understand."

Following are the questions used in the interviews:

Community-Based
1. In what ways do you see the college being community-based?
2. How does the college assess educational needs in the community?
3. How are persons from the community involved in this assessment?
4. How are persons in the community informed of the assessment's findings?
5. How does the college assess community educational resources?
6. How are other institutions and agencies in the community involved in this assessment?
7. How are other institutions in the community informed of the findings?
8. What elements (attitudes, budgets, procedures, etc.) in the college encourage it to be responsive to needs in the community? What elements are constraints?
9. What elements (attitudes, taxes, laws, etc.) in the community encourage the college to be responsive to needs in the community? What elements are constraints?
10. In what way does the college insure that it responds to needs that it discovers in the community?
11. How does the college go about developing (or improving) services?
12. How does the college cooperate with other educational agencies in the community?
13. How does the college serve as coordinator of community

education services offered by itself and other agencies in the community?

14. How do persons in the community participate in establishing or reviewing the college's mission, objectives, and priorities?

15. How are persons in the community informed of the college's mission and objectives?

16. How are persons in the community informed of the college's services?

17. What should the college do to be better aware of and responsive to community needs?

Performance-Oriented

1. In what ways do you see the college being performance-oriented?

2. How does the college evaluate its responses to identified community needs?

3. How are persons from the community involved in this evaluation?

4. How are persons in the community informed of the evaluation findings?

5. How accurate are the evaluations?

6. How accurately are they reported to the community?

7. How well do persons in the community understand the reports?

8. How are community reactions invited? How well received?

9. How does the college act on its own findings? How does it correct deficiencies? How does it set (and reorder) priorities?

10. What elements (attitudes, budgets, procedures, etc.) in the college encourage evaluation of the college's response to community needs? What elements are constraints?

11. What elements (attitudes, taxes, laws, etc.) in the community encourage evaluation of the college's response to community needs? What elements are constraints?

12. How well do persons in the community understand the college's goals and programs? (What *are* the college's goals?)

13. How well and in what ways do persons in the community support the college (taxes, enrollments, volunteer services, etc.)?

14. How (by what means, or on what criteria) do persons in the community form their own informal estimates of the college?
15. How does the college attempt to "read" such informal estimates by persons in the community?
16. What could the college do to obtain a better evaluation of its responses to community needs?

Target-Group Surveys; Advisory Committees. Once the college has analyzed basic information and gathered further information to fill in its picture of the community, it may well discover that some target groups have been overlooked—for example, the aging, the handicapped, dropouts, veterans, unemployed and underemployed, women, those with transportation problems and problems meeting entrance requirements, or those with special training needs. Such a group usually can be reached through target-group survey, which generally is best done through an agency that deals with the group or an advisory committee composed of people who either work with or are themselves members of the group.

Advisory committees operate for various community college programs and are active at many levels, the most common being curriculum development. These committees can be of great help to the college in determining community needs, since their membership usually includes employers and workers in the field represented by the curricular program. The involvement of top-level advisory committees in helping set priorities for programing is recommended. In addition to involving the advisory groups that already exist to deal with the curricular program, establishing target-group advisory committees that deal directly with the community groups for whom educational services may be developed can be extremely helpful.

Finally, it is strongly recommended that a permanent needs-assessment advisory committee be established so that a continuous evaluation of needs-assessment studies can be made. Such a committee requires broad representation, including staff members from as many curricular areas as possible as well as representatives of community groups. The tendency to reject anything "not invented here" exists in any organization, and providing for faculty and staff involvement throughout the needs-assessment process is of utmost importance. Furthermore, the committee can be extremely helpful in coordinating all efforts relating to community-needs assessment.

Predicting Needs

The community renewal college will not develop its programs merely by following currently identified community needs or by reviewing a backlog of needs. Rather, it must charge its staff members explicitly with predicting future needs. These future needs will relate to a variety of educational-services opportunities, such as those that arose from the passage of the Occupational Safety and Health Act. They will derive from the activities of the Environmental Protection Agency and the Federal Energy Commission, as well as those of organizations concerned with the economy, welfare, social security, and the like.

As colleges have attempted to become more community-based, many have developed techniques for analyzing their communities more effectively. The master plan for Brookdale Community College in New Jersey was based on a comprehensive community analysis. More recently, San Diego Community College District has completed a community analysis that has attracted national attention. Seven community colleges in Florida recently joined together in a federally funded consortium to develop better needs-assessment procedures. Central Florida Community College served as the lead college, and each of the others developed a module of the entire project: Florida Junior College at Jacksonville, Valencia Community College, Florida Keys Community College, Brevard Community College, Lake City Community College, and St. Johns River Junior College. The case study that follows describes the contribution of one college in the consortium.

CASE STUDY: FLORIDA JUNIOR COLLEGE AT JACKSONVILLE

Community and junior colleges are capable of meeting a wide variety of community needs. More than any other educational institution, the community college can respond to the need for specialized education in a number of areas, as well as provide the more traditional general education. Accordingly, it is important that the community college keep in touch with community needs, attitudes, and opinions.

In response to this need for information, Florida Junior College at Jacksonville developed a community-survey process which provided the types of information that ensure adequate communication between community and college. This process, as developed and tested in Duval and Nassau counties, Florida, obtained very accurate information in a relatively short time, at an exceptionally low cost.

The problem facing the college was how to obtain an accurate picture of the entire community's attitudes about a wide range of educational issues. The solution as developed involved a random-sampling technique and personal interviews conducted by student interviewers. The college began the initial steps of the survey process on August 1, 1973, and completed the interviewing in late October. A total of 876 interviews were conducted in the two-county area. Following is a step-by-step description of the survey process, beginning with the setting of objectives and ending with a summary of the uses to which the survey results were put.

The first step in the survey process was to determine objectives: what was it that the college needed to know? The choice of objectives should reflect the thinking of a large segment of the college community. Procedures should be established that would ensure input from many sources. A series of meetings with key personnel was desirable. It was also important that the objectives and the survey design be compatible. If the major concern of the college was to obtain an evaluation from former students, a random community survey was not a good design. If the college was concerned about the attitudes of certain population subgroups, such as blacks or non-high-school graduates, methods for sampling only within these groups would have to be found—or, if a communitywide sample was also desired, it would have to be of sufficient size to include subgroup samples large enough to yield statistically reliable projections.

Once the objectives were set and the survey design decided upon, the next step was to ensure that randomness could be achieved and the mechanics of conducting the survey were workable and within cost limitations. The design decided upon was personal interviewing of a communitywide random sample large enough to provide accurate projections for population subgroups. In order to ensure randomness, Bureau of the Census Standard Metropolitan Statistical Area maps were used. A grid was superimposed on the college service area in such a way that each cell had a population of approximately 250. The size of cells varied from census tract to census tract, depending on the population density. Numbering the cells and then consulting a random-number table produced the sample of 250 cells. The intersection nearest the center of each cell was used as the interview location. Four nearby residences were chosen by another randomizing procedure; an interview was to be conducted at each residence. The process described above is a form of multistage cluster sampling.

It was also important to decide how the survey would be conducted. Students were employed as interviewers, using their own cars to get to the interview locations. This system seemed to work well. The best interviewers were those students who already had some interest in fields related to the survey. Emphasis was placed on drawing interviewers from political science, sociology, statistics, or related classes, so that interviewers could relate their survey work to their class work and perhaps use it in a class project. About a third of those hired said they could use their own cars (being reimbursed at the state mileage rate) for the survey. This was ample, since four interviewers were sent to each interview location and the students could conduct four interviews simultaneously.

At the same time the survey capability was being established, the instrument to be used was being designed by a professional consultant from the Community Assessment Laboratory in Columbia, South Carolina. This was a very important step because the usefulness of the entire survey depended directly on the quality of the questionnaire. Extreme care was taken in the wording of the questions. College personnel often use words that have unique meaning for educators; these were avoided. Furthermore, words or expressions can be interpreted differently by different segments of the community. For this reason, the survey had more than one question about each area of concern to reduce the effect of ambiguous questions; this feature also allowed measurement of attitude strengths. The questionnaire contained seventy-seven questions, each uniquely applicable to F.J.C.J. Other college districts tried, without success, to adapt these questions to their own needs.

The Community Assessment Laboratory designed a special computer program capable of analyzing the survey results. The program could calculate absolute and relative frequencies for each answer and analyze subgroups, identified either by a demographic characteristic or by their answers to survey questions.

Another important part of the survey was the employment and training of the interviewers. Hiring of student interviewers began two weeks before the survey was to begin, and a two-day training session was conducted for these students. It was important that the interviewers understand the logic behind the sampling process and the necessity of making the sample selection a random one. On the first day, the theory behind the survey was explained, along with the steps the interviewers would have to follow to locate and conduct each interview. They were also given copies of the questionnaire and allowed to conduct practice interviews among themselves. On the second day, the interviewers were taken into the field, and each conducted an interview under actual survey conditions. Afterward, problems were discussed and questions answered. For interviewers hired after the survey began, the theory and process were explained, and they were sent with an experienced interviewer to conduct their first interview.

The survey was conducted from 4:00 P.M. to 8:30 or 9:00 P.M. on Mondays through Thursdays. This time was selected because it increased the chances of finding a good cross section of people at home. It also was convenient for the interviewers.

Emphasis was placed on interviewers' neatness, the men being required to wear ties and the women to "dress appropriately." Each interviewer wore a badge bearing the college's name and seal, and carried a letter from the president introducing the interviewer and explaining the importance of the survey to the college.

The most rewarding phase of the community-needs-assessment survey has been realized through the use of the survey results. With the assistance of the Community Assessment Laboratory, a final report and analysis was completed for use as a source for making a variety of decisions based on empirical data. For each of the seven survey questions, the data were reported for seventeen subgroups established by five demographic variables: black/white, male/female, veteran status, geographical location, and age (16–19, 20–25, 26–35, 36–54, and 55–older).

The survey has accomplished all the objectives suggested under "Community Awareness and Public Opinion," earlier in this chapter. The data from the survey have guided the college in planning, improving, and expanding the educational programs it offers to the community in the Jacksonville area. The college has expanded a variety of occupational/vocational training programs, such as welding, cabinetwork and millwork, plumbing, pipefitting, steel fabrication, air conditioning and refrigeration, machine shop, X-ray engineering, respiratory therapy, correctional training, legal-paraprofessional training, and occupational-safety training for industry. Programs for adult basic education, high school completion by credit, and high-school-equivalency testing have also been expanded. Special-interest and cultural-enrichment programs are now offered to persons categorized as "aging," through the federally supported program Older Persons Using Skills. (Of course, a variety of courses from yoga to bridge have always been offered to the general public on a self-supporting basis.) In addition, the college opened, in the fall of 1973, a federally supported program known as the Women's Center.

The survey results have helped the college evaluate the effect of its promotional efforts within the community—thus assisting in its effort to provide information to the community. Several significant steps have been taken to improve the accuracy of information that the community has about the college and to provide the information through regular channels of communication. Student Development Offices are now providing counselors for day and evening students who are enrolled in credit and noncredit courses and programs as well as for potential students.

The avenues for providing information have been expanded to include more newspaper articles about new and current programs offered in the curriculum. Probably the most innovative project was a television marathon jointly sponsored by the college and the local educational-television station. For one and a half hours, the cameras showed the variety of programs offered in the college, while counselors, administrators, and other staff members provided accurate, up-to-date information to several thousand callers making inquiries to telephone numbers posted. The response was overwhelming for both the college and the community.

The survey has helped the college remove barriers to attendance. Using the survey data, the college provided the local transportation authority with valuable information as to the need for increased transportation in particular areas of the community. In addition, a new (fourth) campus that emphasizes occupational/vocational programs is under construction in a central urban location. Conditions that impede learning, usually a barrier for attendance or continued attendance, have been identified and staff development initiated in curriculum-development areas such as program and course objectives, varied instructional practices, and mediated instruction. The Student Development Offices have developed study-skills clinics and test-anxiety-desensitization clinics. Barriers related to racial discrimination were, happily, insignificant in affecting attendance.

Finally, the survey has been valuable in evaluating the quality of curricular programs and their impact on the community. Using the survey data, the college planned a follow-up study to determine how well the stated objectives of its programs and courses match the preparation that graduates will need in order to meet requirements for job proficiency. The results of the study will be used to provide "curriculum validation" for successful programs and to recommend changes in course and program objectives.

As we have seen, the community-needs-assessment survey has given Florida Junior College at Jacksonville empirical data that are providing a reliable basis for decision making in developing new programs or altering existing programs; determining appropriate channels for communication of the type of information needed by potential students; removing barriers to attendance; and evaluating the effectiveness of programs and courses in promoting success beyond the college doors.

Community analyses reveal *people's* needs—not such vague requirements as "making our community more beautiful" or "making our community a magnet for new business" or "making our community a mecca for tourists." All these secondary purposes, of course, affect people. But the community renewal college is concerned first with people—with preparing people to take advantage of whatever opportunities come along; helping them develop the skills, attitudes, and knowledge to improve and renew their neighborhoods; lifting them to new heights of educational aspiration; reaching into every corner of their communities, and offering all who live there the opportunity and the know-how to create a new world for themselves and those who surround them.

III

Cooperating with Community Agencies

The commonplace "The only constant is change" is a truism that describes most communities in America today. Community change, like an elevator car, always proceeds in one of two directions: up or down. Unfortunately, in too many communities across the nation, the elevator of change is on its way down, and gathering momentum. Its direction can be reversed, but only if the community, overcoming apathy and uniting as one, can find the will to push the "up" button before the elevator crashes to the bottom of the shaft.

United action, however, is not an attribute with which communities are inherently endowed. Communities are composed of diverse groups and individuals, and these components can seldom be drawn together in a concerted effort to prevent or reverse downward trends—unless a catalyzing agent consolidates and directs their energies. Such a catalyst is the community renewal college. If an

44

institution is to become a community renewal college, its leaders must recognize that the college and the community are interdependent. It seems obvious that the college as an agency does not exist in isolation from the community and its many organizations and agencies, but hundreds of years of carefully guarded tradition impede understanding of that basic reality. For most of the history of higher education, colleges were considered repositories of knowledge to be defended against the intrusion of the outside world. Gradually, colleges became more socially conscious and made direct efforts to provide assistance to their communities, states, or national governments—assistance in the form of research projects, extension services, demonstration units, and, most frequently of all, pompously academic pronouncements on the affairs of the day.

Only within recent years have colleges in any numbers attempted to do more than provide services *to* the community. With the concept of the community renewal college must come the concept of the college as an institution operative *for, in,* and *by* the community—a college that is a vital part of the community rather than one that merely provides services to the community.

The college that has analyzed its community to any extent will have found that the college itself is only one of many organizations with objectives and goals related to community improvement. In fact, many organized forms of adult learning are being sponsored by institutions other than colleges. Most community organizations—whether business, civic, religious, governmental, or special interest—consider it one of their missions to serve not only the special needs of their own client-constituencies but also the broader, public interest of the community. And their missions almost always include educational components: making the client-constituency or the general public more knowledgeable about some topic, more aware of particular needs and concerns, or more skillful in solving particular problems. Hence in every community there is a multiplicity of organizations and agencies involved in community education and renewal —organizations whose objectives include improving the quality of community life.

There are many reasons that a community renewal college should be concerned with the great variety of agencies and organizations in its area. First, such agencies and organizations are important parts of the community. Their needs and their resources are a part of the complex organism that *is* the community, and the community renewal college will develop a relationship with all its parts. Failure to recognize community organizations and their strengths and weaknesses, their resources and needs, their problems and ability to solve problems is to ignore a large and vital part of the community. Failure to establish working relationships with them is failure to work with the total community.

A second and quite pragmatic reason for working with community organizations and agencies is the conservation of valuable college and community resources. Many colleges have found that the needs of the community require services that are costly to administer, and that community services are poorly funded by state and local resources. At the time when many colleges are starting to move into their destined roles as agents for total community education and renewal, economics may be exerting pressure for these same colleges to revert to traditional types of education aimed at traditional types of students. The most effective community renewal colleges will be those that are successful in efforts to maximize their abilities to serve their communities with limited resources.

A third and very important reason for involving the college with the community in cooperative arrangements is that off-campus instruction is sometimes preferable. Its advantages relate to student access and to the need to make learning practical in today's society. Educational programs held in the community will attract students who would not travel to the suburban college, and the learning experiences gained in the community are likely to be more directly related to student and community needs than the typical learning experiences gained on campus.

The benefits to the community when the college and community organizations work together constitute a fourth reason that cooperative efforts should be an important aspect of the college's community renewal program. Involvement of many organizations and agencies in education for a single community, while a great source of strength for community development and improvement, is also a potential source of weakness in that the organizations may be competing for the same public dollars and may be providing the same services independently to the same constituencies. Moreover, some organizations may not be getting the job done or not doing it well. Often there is needless overlapping of responsibilities, duplication of services, and consequent waste of time, energy, talent, and physical and financial resources. Then, too, many organizations and agencies lack adequate facilities, personnel, leadership, finances, knowledge, and expertise in program planning and development.

The independent efforts toward community renewal would undoubtedly be more effective if organizations pooled their resources. Cooperative efforts by the college and those community organizations that have a mutuality of interest could provide services that neither the college nor an organization could accomplish alone. Both could conserve physical and human resources while being more responsive, effective, and efficient in meeting community needs. Such cooperative efforts would maximize the strengths and compensate for the weaknesses of both the college and the community organizations.

As the agency with the broadest base of operations, the community renewal college should take upon itself the task of bringing the many community organizations and agencies into a working relationship. In the words of Myran (1974, p. 15), "It is possible that the community college will no longer play an exclusive role in the community, but rather will be . . . the agency which weaves the fabric of education together wherever it takes place in whatever form."

The direct benefits to the college and to the organizations and agencies of the community constitute a fifth reason for working together. As an agent for community renewal the college has both assets and limitations, which vary from college to college. Each agency or organization within the community has strengths and weaknesses, which make it both a community resource and a prospective beneficiary of the college's efforts to improve the community. The college, by working with community agencies and organizations, can help them become stronger, more effective agents of community renewal while shoring up its own weaknesses with their strengths. A symbiotic relationship can develop in which the strengths of the college and those of various community organizations support and sustain each other. In the long term, the greatest beneficiary will be the community itself.

What are the benefits accruing to the community college from cooperative ventures with community organizations? First, each community organization has intimate knowledge of the needs of one or more constituencies. For this reason, community organizations can play a vital role in the continuing process of community analysis. Beyond the identification of needs, agencies and organizations in the community can help the college plan, implement, and evaluate programs to serve their constituencies. Through advisory committees, joint task forces, liaison relationships, and other types of working arrangements, the college can begin to see the community through the eyes of its representatives.

Organizations have formal and informal channels of communication to their members and to their constituents. These channels provide an organization with a community base, an organizational structure, influential contacts, and an "in" with particular segments of the community that the college may not have. Such channels of communication can give the college a better perspective of the community and a means of publicizing its mission as a community-based institution. Informing the public of its community renewal intent, the services it has to offer, and even the particular programs, courses, and events that it schedules has proved to be one of the most difficult challenges a would-be community renewal college must face. A well-planned program of community services is only as effective as the college's ability to "get the word out" to the community in general or to a particular target group. The process is expensive, time-consuming, and limited in scope when the college works alone; it can be free, fast, and far-reaching when community organizations take it upon themselves to inform their own memberships of college/community activities.

Community agencies and organizations frequently have access to a corps of volunteer workers who are willing to assist with all types of duties from clerical work to canvassing neighborhoods or instructing classes. These dedicated volunteers frequently mean the difference between success and failure for a community project by providing the extra communications effort, the extra office help, or the extra assistance with facilities and logistics. The benefits of an active program of volunteerism, overlooked by many colleges, can be of great importance to the community renewal college. Frequently, an organization will have among its human resources leaders who can become active spokesmen for or organizers of college/community activities. Organizations may have facilities that can be of great help in the combined effort, particularly if the facilities are more accessible either geographically or psychologically to the target groups.

Effective organizations have a momentum of their own which the college could not duplicate with any amount of effort, for the momentum is a sum total of the organization's history, its successes and failures, its goals and motivations, and its membership and leadership. The college can work with the organization to channel this momentum in the direction of jointly selected activities.

The college's and community's images of each other will change as the college begins to work with community groups on a partnership basis. The college will gain a better perspective of one or more publics within its community as it loses its "ivory tower" insularity. The college will gain valuable credibility in the eyes of the community as it demonstrates, rather than talks about, its interest in working with groups, agencies, and organizations for community improvement.

In short, the college attempting to become effectively involved with the community in improvement and renewal activities should recognize the great potential of community organizations and agencies. Through joint ventures the college can utilize the many assets of such groups to extend its services to the community while conserving resources. Many organizations can provide the community renewal college with a vehicle for improving its image as a community-based agency and providing services to many constituencies whose needs it could not meet alone.

What benefits would accrue to community organizations from cooperative ventures with colleges? First, organizations can benefit from the college's understanding of the total community and its broad-based support. Its larger perspective on the community—a perspective that transcends those of many special-interest groups—will enable the college to assist organizations in community-needs assessment. In cooperative ventures many community organizations will benefit from being identified with the image and prestige of the college. Colleges tend to have more diffuse communication networks than special-interest community organizations do. Hence the college can serve as a catalyst in making organizations aware of the particular needs of other organizations' client-constituencies and of each organization's potential for meeting these needs. Moreover, the community college can and should serve as a liaison in linking various community organizations in joint undertakings. The college has facilities, educational expertise, and a professional staff to assist community organizations in developing programs to meet their own needs and the needs of their constituencies. Some organizations may have to draw extensively on the college's facilities, personnel, and resources for support; others may have the necessary facilities, personnel, and resources but lack the expertise and leadership for planning and establishing a program. Here the community renewal college may serve to strengthen a particular organization—to make it more community-based—while indirectly serving the needs of the organization's client-constituency.

Types of Community Organizations

The typical community contains too many types of organizations and agencies for an exhaustive listing. In the following discussion are presented the several types with which colleges are most often involved in joint educational endeavors.

Special Interest. Many, but not all, special-interest groups are appropriate for joint endeavors. There are garden clubs with strong interests in community beautification, ecology-minded groups, such as the Audubon Society and the Sierra Club, and societies with concern for the preservation of the history of the community, state, or region. There are the Daughters of the American Revolution, the Women's Christian Temperance Union, and Alcoholics Anonymous—all with obvious educational objectives. Collectors' organizations abound, such as orchid societies, coin collectors' clubs, and collectors of almost every type of antiques—clocks, musical instruments, dolls, automobiles, books. Most are eager to educate the community about their particular objects of interest. Most offer excellent resource persons as instructors, visiting lecturers, and demonstrators.

Ethnic, Women's, and Related. Although many ethnic organizations have been active in communities for years, recent ethnic
awareness has spawned a host of new organizations. True ethnic
organizations have primary objectives related to their ethnicity—
the promotion, preservation, recognition, or protection of their group
or its culture or traits. This definition excludes special-interest groups
whose membership happens to be of one ethnic group, such as the
neighborhood garden club composed of blacks. Frequently only the
involvement of ethnic organizations can give the college its initial
entree to a particular segment of the community. Joint efforts by
colleges and ethnic organizations may cause the image of the college
to change from "an institution out there, planning to do something
to us" to "someone working with us to achieve our goals."

Women's. Closely akin to ethnic organizations are those dedicated to the causes of other groups of people. The foremost example
of such a group in our present society is women. Organizations range
from the most militant women's-liberation groups to those fighting
women's liberation. Many are dedicated to education. Organizations
like the Council for the Continuing Education of Women in one
community (see the case study later in this chapter) exemplify a
very positive, productive approach, stressing counseling, job training
and placement, continuing education, self-fulfillment, and enrichment. Such organizations make valuable allies. Few organizations
can match the dedication of their members or the tirelessness of
their volunteers.

Social and Civic. Many social and civic organizations have
strong educational or community-improvement objectives. Kiwanis
International, Rotary International, and the JayCees have goals
related to local, national, and international affairs. Women's clubs
such as Junior Sorosis and the Junior League have participated
effectively with colleges in a myriad of community projects. The
volunteer forces mustered by these organizations can be of great help
to the college.

Age. An age organization is one whose purposes and goals
are related to a particular age group, as distinguished from a special-
interest or civic organization whose members tend to be of the same
age. Senior citizens' organizations tend to predominate in this category, since the young and the middle-aged seldom focus on prob-

lems peculiar to their age groups. Perhaps no constituency in the
community needs the help of the community renewal college more
than the elderly. Our changing social and family patterns have left
many of our elderly alone or in communities of aged people. Their
problems related to health, mobility, finances, and employment, as
well as their particular needs for life enrichment, can best be at-
tacked by the college working jointly with organizations able to give
a clear perspective on what it is like to be old.

Health and Social Service. Private organizations such as the
American Cancer Society, the Salvation Army, Alcoholics Anonymous, and Parents of Retarded Children count education of the
general public among their foremost goals. The support in materials,
organization, and programs they bring from their national organizations, as well as their ability to recruit volunteer workers, makes
them ideal partners in community education. Governmental agencies providing social services may be local (such as a human-services
council), state-based (such as a welfare system), or national (such
as Social Security). All are concerned with the solution of community problems and can assist the college with its efforts at community renewal.

Governmental. Cities, counties, and states are agencies with
whom the college can and should cooperate. They have great
varieties of educational needs and interests. City and county agencies
frequently need training for employees and are willing to plan joint
programs. Law enforcement has been the most fruitful area of cooperation to date, because of federal funds. The involvement of
governmental agencies in community analysis is an excellent way to
begin a cooperative relationship. The image of the college as a
service agency for the community will be enhanced by cooperation
with governmental units and their agencies.

Professional and Labor. Practically every profession, craft,
or trade has an organization devoted to the protection, education, or
improvement of its membership. The local bar association and the
local electricians' union, the secretaries' association and the medical
association operate programs directed internally at their membership and externally at the community in general. Liaisons with such
organizations frequently produce training programs. By helping

such organizations communicate with the public through community-service programs, the college can benefit from their prestige and the loyalty of their members.

Neighborhood or Civic Improvement. From the most sophisticated chamber of commerce to the smallest neighborhood-improvement association, a common purpose emerges: the betterment of the community. Chambers of commerce have such breadth of membership and such far-ranging goals and objectives, and they undertake such a great variety of programs, that several pages could be written on the potential areas of cooperation between them and community renewal colleges. Few joint efforts will bring the college into contact with more civic-minded community leaders or involve it in more community projects.

Educational. The college should not overlook other educational organizations and agencies as potential partners in community activities. Public and private schools and colleges are natural allies for the community renewal college. Cooperation may range from a simple sharing of facilities to the undertaking of large community-improvement projects.

Clackamas Community College, in Oregon, has developed an exemplary ongoing relationship with the area's community schools. In 1972, the college board of education approved a proposal to give the college's director of community education the responsibility of working with local public-school districts in developing a plan for cooperation between high schools having adult-education programs in the college district and the community college. It was expected that by the fall of 1974, 80 per cent of the public-school districts in the Clackamas Community College district would be involved in the cooperative community-education program. In the first eighteen months that this program was in existence, all administrative problems were solved to the satisfaction of the college and the local school districts. The college has experienced as much as a 300 percent growth in overall enrollment in college credit classes where the cooperative arrangements with the local school districts exist. Through joint planning, the college and its surrounding school districts have arrived at the following delineation of responsibilities (Tucker, 1974–1975):

The Community College

Offers college courses, both credit and noncredit, to all who can benefit from them.

Offers courses and activities that are not part of the community school programs.

Offers a wide range of occupational and lower-division transfer-credit courses in addition to adult/community-education courses.

Assigns staff members as consultants for facilitators to community schools.

Offers services to community schools even when the community college personnel are not explicitly asked by community school administrators.

Has tuition and fees that are different from community schools' fees.

Is responsible for community education in the parts of its district where there are no community school programs.

Develops training programs for paraprofessionals, community school directors, coordinators, and related personnel.

Community Schools

Offer courses appropriate to their local communities only.

Offer programs different from the community college's even when community schools are in locations far from the community college.

Offer courses and programs that are flexible in length, in starting dates, and in class hours taught.

Utilize volunteer and nonvolunteer instructors regardless of whether they are certified.

Allow people from other communities to participate in local community schools' programs and activities when there is available space.

Business. Although technically not organizations in the sense in which the word has been used in this chapter, businesses in the community are too important to omit in any discussion of community college liaisons with community agencies. The fact that businesses are motivated by (among other things) profit is no obstacle to cooperation with them. Businesses provide employment for citizens; businesses support the community; and in their public-relations endeavors, businesses provide many community benefits. Businesses need training of employees and are generally willing to pay for it.

They generally value the association with educational institutions and can often provide the college with resources such as funds, facilities, and expertise.

Northern Virginia Community College has developed a unique cooperative venture with IBM Corporation that involves flexible scheduling, the development of innovative programs, and a willingness on the part of the college to take programs into factories where workers are. Cooperation with IBM has brought requests for educational programs from many other businesses and organizations in the area.

Modes of Cooperation with Community Agencies

Modes of cooperation between the community renewal college and community organizations range from casual contacts to complete mergers. The type of relationship developed depends upon what is perceived as possible and desirable by the college and the community organization. This is determined by the type of organization involved, its mission, and its resources. Obviously, both the college and the organization must perceive a mutuality of interests and benefits for any association to persist. For purposes of analysis, it is possible to look at four distinct modes of cooperation, even though a continuing relationship with an organization will likely involve several modes, the relationship shifting from one mode to another as needs dictate.

Advisory Relationships. The advisory mode is the most common college/community relationship. The use of community advisory committees by colleges is more frequent, but a community-based college will find itself and its people used more and more as advisers to community organizations as its interest in the community and its potential for assistance become more widely known. The advisory relationship may be temporary, for a project of short dura-ation, or long-range, for a continuing college program.

Because the advisory arrangement is the simplest and most common mode of cooperation between the college and the community, it has great value that should not be underrated. The college that has developed every type and degree of cooperating relationship with community organizations will still rely heavily on the use of representatives of agencies and organizations as advisers.

Direct Assistance. Direct assistance is the provision of services or of facilities, expertise, or other resources in a way that is directly involved in the carrying out of the educational endeavor. Like advisory assistance, direct assistance may pass from the college to the community organization or vice versa. For example, a college may provide a course for an agency, or an organization may provide facilities for a college. Such arrangements may be for any length of time determined by the nature of the project. They are usually more formal than advisory relationships and should be spelled out in a contract if funds, personnel, or similar resources are involved. Direct-assistance arrrangements are common when organizations want to serve particular constituencies but do not have the resources or expertise to undertake the task immediately, whereupon they contract for services from the community college. The reciprocal form of the relationship is of benefit to the college in need of a service that can be offered by an existing community agency, when instituting a program to provide the service within the college would result in needless duplication, overlapping of programs, and waste of resources. For example, a local bank might provide office space for a college music department to sell concert tickets, and not charge rent for this service.

Joint Ventures. Joint ventures are truly cooperative arrangements: in them, the college and an organization or agency work together in an educational enterprise. Joint-venture arrangements are also more formal than advisory relationships, and a contract should spell out the duties and obligations of each party, preventing misunderstandings as the project develops. The choice of techniques that will be effective in a joint venture will vary greatly with the organization involved and the relationship sought. In an ideal joint venture each party's strengths will complement the other's weaknesses. Joint ventures require that each organization have some knowledge about the other and, above all, mutual respect for the other's capabilities and purposes.

Mergers. Finally, a legal arrangement that may become more common as community renewal colleges develop is a merger of the college and a community organization. In a merger both the college and the organization, perceiving themselves to have common interests with respect to a particular targeted constituency, contract to pool their resources in a long-term cooperative enterprise in which each bears specified responsibilities and shares in the benefits. The contract for the merger spells out the roles of the individuals involved, and the responsibilities of the college and the community organization. In many respects this is the optimal relationship; the community agency and the college achieve complete symbiosis: in providing services to a constituency that neither could adequately serve alone, they share the expenditure of resources, the benefits, and the credit. Since most colleges are public bodies unable to give up their identities, a community organization more often becomes an arm of a college than the reverse.

Forming Liaisons with Community Organizations

Before a community renewal college decides to enter into a working arrangement with a community organization, it should assess the characteristics of the organization. This is necessary in order to determine whether the organization offers potential for a viable, productive relationship and what the most effective type of arrangement is. Such an investigation should include the following:

1. The objectives of the organization, and their order of priority. What are the hidden, or tacit, objectives, as distinct from the manifest, or stated, objectives? Are the objectives consistent with present commitment of resources?
2. The nature of the constituency. Does serving the targeted constituency fall within the purview or mission of the community renewal college? Can the college respond effectively to meet the needs of the constituency? Is bilateral planning preferable to unilateral planning?
3. The effectiveness of the organization. How effective has the organization been in meeting its objectives in the past? What support do the members give to the leaders and the objectives?
4. The resources of the organization. What are the physical and human resources of the organization—the personnel, time, energy, expertise, facilities, and money? How efficiently has

it used its resources in the past? How much is it willing to commit to a joint venture? Is this an adequate commitment of resources?

5. Leadership in the organization. Who are the most influential and powerful leaders in the organization, and what is their style of leadership? How responsive and responsible are the leaders to the members? How are decisions made? How creative and innovative are the leaders? How effective is their leadership with the targeted constituency? What are the leaders' attitudes about sharing resources, benefits, and, most of all, the credit or prestige from a joint venture?

6. Communication within the organization, and between the organization and its constituency. What are the internal and external channels of communication? What channels are provided for feedback from the constituency? What does the feedback reflect about the adequacy of the organization's performance?

Needless to say, it is equally important that the community organization know the answers to the same questions about the college.

A clear, concise statement of the cooperative arrangements, based on thorough analyses of the community organization and the college, must be developed. As implied in "Modes of Cooperation," above, the more involved and permanent these arrangements are, the more detailed and legalistic the contract should be. Advisory relationships are most often simply confirmed by letter. Direct assistance (if more than a temporary offering of expertise)', joint ventures and mergers should be based on formal contracts. The contractual agreement should be developed bilaterally and should specify at least the following:

1. Source of funds. How much and from whom?
2. Budget. How are funds allocated? Who approves spending?
3. Governing structure. Who is in charge? What is the relation of the leadership of the college to the leadership of the organization? Who makes what decisions? At what level?
4. What services will be supplied, by whom, when, and where?
5. What are the objectives of the project, and how will evaluation be conducted?

6. Who has the many responsibilities of communication, supervision, recruitment, and so forth?
7. What are the conditions for termination of the contract? How will jointly owned resources be disposed of?

Before entering into formal arrangements with a community organization, the community renewal college must be willing to share with the organization many aspects of administration that the college may have previously considered solely its prerogatives. The college should be able to answer affirmatively the following questions.

Is the college willing to share in the planning of the project? Community organizations will want to feel that they are involved in a partnership. Many college administrators will find the joint planning process difficult and time-consuming.

Is the college willing to share the leadership function and the decision-making function? A truly cooperative arrangement will involve both parties in various degrees of leadership and decision making. The college must decide whether and to what degree these functions can be shared. Some administrative functions must by state or local law remain with a public college.

Is the college willing to share responsibility? The college must decide to what extent it wishes to give up responsibility for any educational enterprise in which it is involved (except as the law requires it to retain responsibility). Community agencies will want to feel that they have some responsibility for the ongoing activity.

Last, and perhaps most difficult, is the college willing to share the credit for successes? It is extremely important that community agencies that depend on their membership or on the community for support receive credit for joint activities. Many times it is best for the organization to receive most or all of the credit. In such cases there are usually other benefits to the college more important than the short-lived publicity. The college will add to its image as a community renewal college, and the goodwill of that organization toward the college will spread to other organizations in the community.

There are many examples of two- and four-year colleges that have found ways to meet the needs of their communities more effectively by working with community organizations and agencies. Mott Community College, in Flint, Michigan, was a pioneer in the development of cooperative relationships with public schools and other community agencies as part of the community school movement. And Delaware County Community College, in Media, Pennsylvania, has a close working relationship with the Delaware County area vocational/technical schools, including articulation agreements and contracted educational services in such courses as Foods, Welding, and Dental Assisting. The college has attempted to develop programs and services within the range of its mission according to the assessed needs of the community it serves. The assessment of need is through various means, including direct relationships with school boards (sponsors) and school administrators, involvement of various public agencies, and representation of the community on various advisory committees of the college. The fact that more than thirty agencies are cooperating with the college in identifying needs and developing programs of continuing education and community services attests to the college's efficacy as a coordinator and its responsiveness to community need in providing educational opportunities.

CASE STUDY: VALENCIA COMMUNITY COLLEGE

Since its beginning in 1967, Valencia Community College, in Orlando, Florida, has worked closely and cooperatively with hundreds of community organizations and agencies in carrying out its mission as a community-based, community renewal college. The college has used a variety of modes of cooperation in establishing working relationships with community organizations to assess community educational needs, establish and implement programs, and evaluate their effectiveness. These relationships, in fact, have included all four modes of cooperation discussed earlier in this chapter —advisory relationships, direct assistance, joint ventures, and mergers. Some of the relationships have shifted from one mode of cooperation to another as needs have changed.

The advisory mode allows cooperation on a temporary or continuing basis. Advisory committees are frequently used to determine needs within certain constituency groups. For example, the

Continuing Education for Nurses program at the college receives input from nurses representing nearby hospitals and the state nursing association. Advisory committees are also required to meet the specifications of many federal grants. In developing the proposal for the Emergency Medical Technology program, the college used several advisory groups; their members included firemen, doctors, nurses, and hospital administrators. In cooperation with the national office of the Institute of Lifetime Learning, local senior citizens' groups assisted the college in establishing the Central Florida Institute of Lifetime Learning.

The college also serves in an advisory role to many community organizations. Since gaining a reputation as a community-based organization, the college has frequently been contacted by other organizations for advice and support. A local chapter of the Alpha Kappa Alpha sorority each year plans a series of community-service activities, including a career clinic for high school students, a soul-food festival, and a black business fair. The college is asked to provide leadership and public-relations support in organizing these events. In many instances initial requests result in the establishment of lasting cooperative projects. Epicenter, an interdenominational religious institution, asked the college for advice in developing a course for divorced persons. This program has been conducted successfully by Epicenter. The college is also assisting Epicenter in the development of a booklet for the recently divorced.

The college is frequently asked to provide direct assistance to various community organizations. Volunteer organizations generally operate on a small scale and lack needed resources. The Adult Literacy League, for example, has been provided office space and equipment at the college, and it has received support from the college's public-relations staff. Many small businesses do not have the resources to conduct in-service training. Local businessmen representing the Florida Pest Control Association suggested that the college develop a series of courses to provide basic skills for trainees in their field. The college designed and taught three such courses, aided by the expertise of representatives from the association.

The college frequently needs facilities and equipment. Nearby hospitals have provided facilities and staff time to assist in the training of nurses and Emergency Medical Technicians. The

Lions Clubs of Central Florida have donated a twenty-four-pas-
senger bus, with wheelchair lift, for use in a program for the handicapped; Civil Defense has made available an emergency vehicle.
Many other organizations provide classroom space throughout the
community where courses can be conducted.

An example of a joint venture on a continuing basis is the
relationship between Valencia and the Junior Sorosis, a young
women's social and service club. In the fall of 1970, Valencia
sought advisory assistance from the Junior Sorosis of Orlando to
help establish a student's volunteer-service organization. As a result
of this association, Operation Student Concern was established at the
college to help students locate opportunities for volunteer community service related to their course work or their career aspirations.
In the meantime, Junior Sorosis established its own Volunteer Service Bureau. In 1972, Valencia and Junior Sorosis, through the
Volunteer Service Bureau, developed and offered a course in volunteer administration for social-service volunteers in the area.

The close cooperation and mutual assistance of Junior Sorosis and Valencia in the establishment of the Volunteer Service
Bureau and Operation Student Concern helped Junior Sorosis acquire a $10,000 award in the National Community Improvement
Program Competition sponsored by Sears Roebuck and Com-
pany. Following a thorough analysis of many community problems
and needs, Junior Sorosis passed on the $10,000 grant to the Parent
Education Project at Valencia Community College. In November
1973, Junior Sorosis and Valencia entered into a joint venture to
meet the child-development needs of parents in the community. The
two institutions signed an agreement whereby Junior Sorosis would
support the project with the grant and 5,000 volunteer hours annually, and Valencia would provide staffing, facilities, and support
services for the project.

Since the beginning of the joint venture, the Parent Education Project has expanded its undertakings from its first Parent
Co-op Child Care Center (established in March 1974) to a wider
range of parent-education facilities, including additional co-ops
(January 1975) and the Infant Stimulation Laboratory (October
1975) at Florida Hospital. Workshops, seminars, and other activities have been provided for over 2,000 parents since March 1974.

More recently, Junior Sorosis and Valencia established the **Parent Resource Center**, an independently chartered, nonprofit agency with a community-based board of directors. Although neither Junior Sorosis nor Valencia will own the Center, both will give it important support.

The joint venture between the Junior Sorosis and Valencia resulted in the development of effective techniques of cooperation that changed what had been a very general community-service orientation of Junior Sorosis to one in which 90 percent of its service activity was directed toward parent education. The college and Junior Sorosis developed solid community support for the program through joint appearances before various community groups and agencies (which also proved helpful in needs assessment). As a result, a network was established to decentralize parent-education services by establishing them in over sixty locations in the community. Social coffees for Junior Sorosis members provided opportunities for building Parent Education Project support among the organization's membership.

Through their joint venture in the Parent Education Project, Junior Sorosis and Valencia were able to complement each other's strengths and weaknesses in providing a service to the community. Junior Sorosis provided much of the money, thousands of volunteer hours, political contacts, and leadership for the project. Valencia provided staffing, expertise, facilities, supplies and equipment, and, by lending to the project the status and reputation that the college enjoyed in the community, enhancement of public image. Through joint venture as a mode of cooperation, each party provided a service to the community that it could not have effectively provided alone.

The history of Valencia's cooperative relationship with the Council for Continuing Education for Women (ccew) shows how one mode of cooperation can evolve into another. ccew was established as an independent corporation in 1967, the same year the college was organized. In January 1968, ccew asked the college to offer a course on effective listening. By offering this course, Valencia provided direct assistance in helping a community organization meet a specific educational need for its clientele.

In 1969, the president of ccew was asked to become a member of Valencia's Career Advisory Committee, and the college and CCEW cosponsored a course called "Teaching Wives To Be Widows," whose name was later changed to "The Woman Alone." Offering this course represented a joint venture by CCEW and Valencia. Essentially, Valencia was the fiduciary agent, receiving registration fees and paying instructors' salaries and other expenses in the course. CCEW assumed the role of publicizing the course and recruiting students.

At this stage in the evolution of the cooperative relationship, the college not only provided direct assistance to CCEW in offering courses for its clientele but also joined with CCEW in a joint venture to serve the needs of what was perceived to be the common clientele of the two organizations. In addition, during this time CCEW was called upon on many occasions for input into educational matters at the college concerning women—so it was also acting in an advisory role as the college sought to develop programs to fill women's educational needs.

In 1970, Valencia extended direct assistance in helping CCEW develop a grant application and submit it to Title I for funding support. Beginning in 1971, for several years Valencia was listed among the institutional sponsors in the metropolitan area for CCEW. In 1972, Valencia and CCEW jointly developed and submitted another application for funding under Title I, this time to establish a Center for Continuing Education for Women in downtown Orlando. Following the grant award, a merger agreement was drawn up between CCEW and Valencia. The agreement specified that Valencia would provide matching funds for the grant and also the staff, equipment, and facilities for the center. CCEW would provide leadership, publicity, community outreach, and hundreds of hours of volunteer work by its members.

Through the establishment of the Center for Continuing Education for Women, two autonomous organizations combined to establish a program whose activities were designed to further their common goals. The merger was not of two organizations into a third organization, but rather of two autonomous organizations' activities into one combined program to serve their common interest with respect to a particular clientele. The legal contract that established the Center for Continuing Education for Women spells out the responsibilities of ccew and the college. Since the founding of the Center for Continuing Education for Women, ccew and Valencia, through the center, have cooperatively offered eighty-nine courses to more than 1,500 students, counseling to more than 4,000 women in the community and special programs to more than 6,000 women.

Since 1967, the cooperative relationship of ccew and Valencia Community College has evolved from direct assistance through advisory activities and joint ventures into, finally, a merger. Most of the activities of ccew are now connected in some way with the college, yet ccew maintains its autonomy and its image as a volunteer organization in the community. This arrangement illustrates what was referred to earlier in the chapter as a symbiotic relationship between a college and a community organization.

The term "community renewal college" implies, more than anything else, a relationship between the college and the community in which both work together for total community renewal and improvement—a relationship in which the college draws its strength and its direction from the community. Certainly in such an environment one would find many ongoing relationships between the college and various community groups. The college seeks out appropriate agencies and organizations to work with and through in its efforts to serve the community. In turn, as the community begins to perceive the college as a partner in its renewal, the college will be sought out by agencies and organizations. The true community renewal college will join forces with organizations in the community whenever alliances are possible, realizing that through such arrangements the abilities of the college to serve the community will be multiplied manyfold.

IV

Making Programs
Accessible

Learning is a national resource, and the need for learning—intermittent, recurring, and lifelong—has never been greater. But the learners of today are a very different breed from those of a decade or so ago. Not only their needs in learning have changed, but their tastes in learning, as well; and, with few exceptions, postsecondary education has not kept pace. The steady push toward an egalitarian social philosophy; the now blurred limits of the so-called college years; the bafflement of employed persons concerning what to do with increased leisure time; the wasteful (often tragically so) early-retirement pattern: these and other outside pressures are creating new student clienteles and causing postsecondary education to shift from institutional goals to learner goals. There is no question that the learning market exists;

the issue is how to reach it, how best to serve it, and how to ensure that it has access to the college.

Newsweek reported in its April 26, 1976, cover article, "Who Needs College?":

College administrators think now is the time to start persuading the public of something they themselves have long believed: that higher education should not be limited to—much less dominated by—students just out of high school. Campuses, they think, should become centers for lifelong learning. Many schools are opening their doors to adults, encouraging them to come back for retraining when they need it or further education when they want it. At Mundelein College in Illinois, a two-year-old "weekend college" typifies this move to continuing education. Every Friday night 430 adults—full-time workers in the Chicago area—congregate at the school to take courses. They range in age from nineteen to fifty-nine, and their reasons for attending span everything from the desire to escape sheer boredom to the wish to upgrade already established careers. If they want to, they can go to Mundelein just for the fun of it. But with steady attendance, they can earn a Bachelor of Arts degree.

In the past, if students did not take the initiative and apply for admission to college immediately after high school, it was assumed that they had no desire for, and could not profit from, further education. In consequence, student-recruitment efforts were confined almost exclusively to the upper percentiles of high school graduating classes. It is true that community colleges remained available for a variety of other students who sought the benefits of postsecondary education. However, even the community colleges did little to seek out still other learners. The recent decrease in students graduating from high school has caused both colleges and universities to recruit actively among the ranks of so-called nontraditional students. Even today, however, recruitment for most institutions means attracting students to the same programs that the college has always offered.

For example, Lambuth College, in Jackson, Tennessee, has increased its enrollment by over 5 percent each year since 1973, when it abandoned its 143-year-old tradition of offering only liberal arts and began to examine the community around it. It found a need for a program in hotel and restaurant management, which it operates in cooperation with Holiday Inns, Inc. The college has also moved into interior design, industrial management, and computer science. Lambuth College is serving the needs of its students and its community and is flourishing when many traditional liberal-arts institutions are withering in ivory-tower insularity.

To the community renewal college there will be no traditional and therefore no nontraditional students. The people of the community in all their diversity will be the students of the college. There will be no need to recruit in the sense of luring students to the college, when the college and the community work together to assess the learning needs of the community, to plan programs to develop competencies needed by the community, and to develop community-wide awareness of the potential of the college for meeting those needs. A greater concern of the community renewal college will be making certain that the programs of the college are accessible to those for whom they have been developed—accessible not only geographically but in terms of the prospective student's available time, particular learning strengths and weaknesses, previously acquired competencies, attitudes toward learning, and a variety of other conditions that affect the student's access to education.

Typical of programs tailored to particular groups of nontraditional students is the Richmond Center for the Deaf, a program offered by J. Sargeant Reynolds Community College at its downtown campus in Richmond, Virginia. Educational opportunities, coupled with the necessary supportive services, help to fulfill the center's objectives of bridging the gap between community service agencies and the deaf population and providing rehabilitative and continuing-education opportunities to deaf adults. An open-door policy allows deaf persons seeking help to come to the center without an appointment; interpreting assistance and counseling are available. Topics such as "The Law and the Deaf" are dealt with in workshops designed to meet the needs of the area's deaf population. In order to heighten community awareness of and responsiveness to the problems of the deaf, the center offers seminars on deafness and classes in sign language.

Providing access to competency-developing situations, then, is a major responsibility of those who administer the community renewal college. The success or failure of the college will depend on their ability to provide access by establishing appropriate policies, providing adequate financial support, developing an effective organization, securing a qualified staff, and creating the variety of delivery systems needed by the diverse students of the college.

Establishing Policy

To whom does the college that seeks to bring about community renewal really belong? This question must continually be placed before the college staff as well as those in whom the constituency places its trust—the policy makers. The community-based college ultimately belongs to the community, and the local governing board is that body in whose trust the constituency has placed the college to ensure that the purposes of the institution are fulfilled. The policy makers in their role as the trustees of the college are accountable to the community.

Since the policy makers are the first-line contact between the college and the community, they have the prime responsibility for making and keeping the institution community-based and fulfilling its renewal purposes. A board of trustees can easily busy itself with chores such as purchasing, hiring and firing, approving new buildings, and amending the budget. However, its true benefit to the community lies in its ability to establish policies that deal with the purposes of the institution, with the curriculum as it relates to the budget, and with planning based on community needs.

The policy makers of the community renewal college must continually look in two directions: into the college and outside it. They must constantly keep before the administration and faculty the basic purposes of the institution, and, at the same time, hold up these basic purposes to the college's constituent community. The purposes must be studied, delineated, and verbalized continually in order to clarify the college's policies for meeting community needs. The entire idea of community renewal presents a wealth of subject matter to ponder in shaping the purposes of the institution. What are the special characteristics that make a college unique? How successful is the college in achieving its unique purposes? Such questions should haunt the policy maker.

The philosophy of the community-based college as embodied

in the concept of community renewal places an obligation upon its policy makers to see that the institution entrusted to them focuses on the true needs of its community. Some strategies for analyzing community needs have been described in Chapter Two; it should be pointed out again how important it is that governing boards be involved in the process, for only in that way can they become fully aware of community needs and see clearly their responsibilities for meeting those needs. Beyond the formal needs-analysis process, the governing board should provide a continuous flow of feedback from the community to the college.

The trustees are citizens of the community. Perhaps they are members of the business community or the professions; they may also be members of societies, subcultures, or ethnic and other minorities. They represent various alliances with all kinds of people. The board of trustees is a prime sounding board for information gathered about the community. It can validate the results of community-needs analyses. The setting of priorities for the institution, based on the recognized needs, should occupy the policy makers in considerable deliberation. This is not to imply that the staff should abdicate its responsibility for developing recommendations for the policy makers' action. Indeed, it must provide even more leadership focusing upon the future of community renewal for the institution.

When the policy makers of the community renewal college approve the budget and curriculum, they give tangible support to the college's purposes and priorities for their community. When the trustee casts his ballot on budgetary and curricular matters, he exercises his responsibility for the institution entrusted to him by the constituent community. The policy maker who desires his college to become a community renewal college will become extensively involved in budget making. He will not become bogged down in the detailed process of developing the budget at the departmental level; that and similar routine activities are clearly the province of the college staff. Rather, he will continually put forth the questions: How does the budget support the priorities established to meet the needs of this community in order to renew it? If occupational training is a high priority, does the budget show a substantial increase for it? If community services are a high priority, does the budget reflect that fact? He should ask similar questions when considering the curriculum. When the policy maker is satisfied with responses to such questions, he then votes the necessary tools and resources for the college staff to implement renewal for the community.

Administrators for the most part did not predict the enrollment sag of the early seventies. Perhaps policy makers, if given involvement in long-range and contingency planning, could have predicted the change in enrollment patterns. Much of the time, policy makers are so smothered with papers and reports that they have little opportunity for creative planning and projection. It would appear very important for the policy maker to become more involved in creating long-range plans for his constituency. The members of the governing board have probably lived longer with the constituency than either the administrators or the faculty members have. Besides, the policy maker has in his charge the long-term welfare of the institution; concern for long-range decisions, and activities related to such decisions, is therefore likely to be of considerable importance to him. When trustees are involved in long-range and contingency planning, they may be able to see more clearly their roles as agents of change.

The board members must continue to make short-range decisions, because these too should contribute to community renewal. But the members should try to de-emphasize routine matters so that they will have time to probe policy questions related to the true purposes of the institution. Routine duties are not the important reason for the existence of the board. Though the board is obliged by law to accomplish such duties, its responsibility to the community is to bring about changes that will help the institution meet the community's needs.

At each meeting the policy makers should insist on the discussion of broad policy questions related to the welfare of the community. A good way to set the stage for such discussion is to have a slide show, a study, or some other presentation (which will also inform the board of how well the institution is fulfilling its purposes).

Administering for Accessibility

Organizing personnel and support services to promote community access is ultimately the responsibility of the college administration. Administration has been called "the ordering of means to ends" in the total educational enterprise. Unless the community renewal college's administrative and support staffs fulfill their purposes, the instructional and allied activities that can help renew the community will not be properly effected.

All administrative activities should be based on a commitment to the mission of the institution—a commitment that should have evolved from all the information-gathering techniques, community-needs analyses, and interactions with the community that are possible. Specific objectives for administration and support must be derived from the mission statement of the college. Administrative activities should be developed into competency language. Just as the instructional process should not become entangled in a web of paperwork, neither should administrative objectives. They should be to the point, goal-oriented, and related to a variety of activities and conditions, including the following:

1. Facilitating learning. Just as barriers must be removed so that students can have access to the institution and its resources, so must the barriers to the delivery of educational services be removed. The basic responsibility for such removal lies with the administrative organization.

2. Encouragement of change. Administrative effort should always be directed toward creating a climate for innovation and for venturing into new territory. Incentives should be developed to encourage activities that focus on community renewal.

3. Governance. The entire governance system should provide a form of renewal for the college itself and all of its staff. Rigidity in the governance process can impede the college's trying out new roles in the community. Governance should never stand in the way of meeting real community needs. Interminable procedures for changing the curriculum are antithetical to timely response to new needs.

4. Distribution of decision making. Barriers are inherent in a chain of command that removes the locus of decision making too far from the actual learning situation. Close-to-the-scene decisions are usually best. Control of the overall direction of the community renewal effort, however, belongs with top administration. Much autonomy should be given to individ-

uals directly involved in renewal programs, the administrative organization carefully orchestrating the whole.

5. Budgeting. It does little good to establish priorities and missions if the budgeting process is not directed toward renewal of the institution as well as renewal of the community. Management must demonstrate its competencies in weighing priorities against budgetary limitations.

6. Support for the student. If the college organization impedes accommodation and support of the diversity of students served by the community renewal college, then it must be changed. Counseling, registration, financial aid, student activities, placement—all must be available to all clients in the community. The college must expect that it will not be as easy to reach the total community with such services as to reach the traditional student.

7. Support of the instructional process. This must be the top priority of the administration. The community renewal college will of necessity be involved in innovative instructional programs, and the diverse needs of students will mandate highly individualized delivery systems. The administration will need to encourage the faculty to experiment—and support the faculty's efforts with arrangements for time, adequate finances, facilities and equipment, and, above all, praise and recognition.

8. Community input. Administration and support areas must be responsible for facilitating analysis of and interaction with the community. Specific competencies in dealing with advisory committees and community organizations must be developed and evaluated regularly.

9. Organizational development and climate. The continued efforts to improve the organization's climate and to humanize the entire community renewal process from within and without must be facilitated by the administrative and support areas.

Administrative competencies in all the above areas must be tested through an ongoing appraisal system. Efforts that fall short must be analyzed and modified.

Many discussions focus on the pros and cons of the various organizational structures developed to provide more outreach to the community. For example, open colleges and open campuses and noncampuses have been developed in order to facilitate community renewal.

Portland Community College, in Oregon, has developed a community-based "educational shopping center," its Rock Creek Center. It is situated in a new community and is becoming the focus for many activities of the citizens. Many services are provided to all citizens of the community, whether or not they enroll in classes or programs. Some businesses and government services operate out of the center, and their proximity enhances many related career programs. Like the modern shopping center, Rock Creek is customer-oriented. It has an open door, and all programs and activities are highly visible. Open seven days a week from early morning to late at night, it delivers the educational services that people want and need. Students may enter at any time, leave when they have completed their objectives, and reenter when they feel they need more education. They may receive a diagnostic "X ray" of their educational needs, strengths, and weaknesses. Continuous progress through a program allows students to complete course requirements at their own rate. A drive-in information center will make it possible to get information on classes and programs, along with sample units, without leaving the car.

At the same time, community renewal has been facilitated through the normal campus organization of some community colleges. Renewal philosophy and commitment override structure. That philosophy and commitment must begin with the governing board, the president, and other key leaders, and then must pervade the entire institution. Listening to and analyzing the community and then developing programs in cooperation with the community must become a habit for each program leader. The basic organizational structure selected will vary with the needs of the particular community.

Funding Community Renewal

Adequate funding is perhaps the most obvious and, at least on the surface, the most formidable barrier confronting the college that would become a community renewal college. No states and few local systems have funded from tax monies the total array of programs, activities, and services implicit in the term *community re-newal college.* Experience and research have demonstrated that the adequacy of public funding for college programs is in direct proportion to the traditionality of the programs. Most states and localities will fund almost any program that will be conducted as a credit course. Many will fund a program conducted as a noncredit course if the objectives of the program relate to work. Almost none will fund a community program not conducted as a course at all or conducted as a noncredit course with objectives related to enrichment or recreation.

It is easy to understand the reasons underlying these limitations on funding, given the historical development of postsecondary education. Governing bodies composed of laymen, communities, and, indeed, the preponderance of educators hold very traditional views of the objectives of postsecondary education. The term *postsecondary education* itself is of recent coinage and is only now beginning to be used interchangeably with the term *higher education.* For most of our history higher education has implied credit and degrees. Even community colleges, long heralded as the colleges for all the people, considered themselves junior colleges in the most traditional sense of the word for most of their history. Only in recent years has the term *community* begun to replace *junior* and only in recent years have community colleges begun to view more than credits and degrees as valid objectives.

Before community renewal, in all its aspects, can be deemed worthy of public support, those who govern and fund higher education will have to overcome their narrow view of the mission of postsecondary education. This view is elitist in the sense that it has deemed it more acceptable to spend public funds on the student who can achieve the most; it causes education to be aimed primarily at the young, under the assumption that education should be preparation for life rather than a process carried on throughout life; and it is biased toward education that leads to a degree or prepares the student for work, ignoring the values inherent in self-improvement, enrichment, and recreation.

While much remains to be done to secure funding for the total program of the community renewal college, the colleges committed to community renewal need not wait (and, indeed, many are not waiting) for such funding. That innovative ways can be found to fund programs not publicly supported is clear when one compares colleges within a system. Some colleges cite lack of public funds as the reason for not becoming involved in community renewal activities; others with identical public support are heavily involved in such activities.

There are many ways to support community renewal activities without direct state or local funding. Perhaps the most obvious and widespread is the use of federal funds. Since many federal programs are aimed at improving the lot of an individual constituency within the community, solving community problems, testing experimental programs, or some combination of these goals, they relate directly to the work of the community renewal college. The college with creative management and many ties to the community will find it possible to take advantage of not only those federal programs directly related to education but also those aimed at community improvement generally and only indirectly related to education. A note of caution should be given at this point. No college should build its programs solely on federal funds with the expectation of continued federal support. The availability of funds varies greatly from year to year, and they are usually intended as seed money to initiate programs for which the college will ultimately become fiscally responsible. Federal funds can, however, help the college begin programs and allow it to show its community and its lay governing bodies the value of community renewal.

Many colleges have taken the attitude that some courses and activities should help support others. A prestige course offered to a wealthy social stratum in the community might carry a much higher fee than necessary in order to gain funds that can be used to offer a course or a service below cost to another constituency. This arrangement is no different from the customary funding of academic programs. Low-cost lecture courses in the social sciences have always supported costly laboratory courses in the natural sciences.

Cooperation with organizations and agencies within the community will conserve the college's resources and extend its effectiveness. The creative community-based college will find many sources of underwriting for programs and services. Businesses, governmental units, media, foundations, professional associations, other organizations, and individuals—all have interests in promoting various types of programs. The college that knows its community resources will gain support and funding from many areas.

Those colleges already involved in any degree of community renewal, using whatever funding arrangements they can develop, are performing an extremely valuable service for all colleges and deserve special commendation. The value of community renewal will have to be demonstrated before it can be understood, articulated, and given priority in public support. Eventual acceptance of the community renewal mission of the community-based college will require a long-range plan of dissemination of information. The basic concepts of community service, community-based education, and, ultimately, the community renewal college must be articulated and communicated to other educators so that the problems and potentials will be widely understood. Until a majority of educators understand and accept the goals of community renewal, it cannot be expected that the community and lay governing bodies will understand those goals and give them priority in public policy and funding. Educators already involved in community renewal need to take an active role in communicating to their colleagues elsewhere the value of their programs. The variety of programs and the resulting benefits to communities can be communicated through literature, through involvement of colleges in consortia, and through our national community college organizations.

One of the major problems in explaining community renewal programs—and one of the major reasons that public policy makers have not given these programs a high priority—is that the majority of "new students" whom the community renewal college hopes to reach are not aware of the potential benefits of the college, nor are they organized to communicate their wishes and needs to the proper authorities. There is much cooperative work to be done between colleges and communities in explaining their missions and in demonstrating the benefits of community renewal. The college must also assist the various constituencies in its community to organize themselves and to make it known to college boards of trustees and state legislators that they have educational needs as important and pressing as those of any other segment of society.

Leaders in community renewal must take an active role in

informing various levels of lay governing bodies about the need for
the renewal enterprise. They must show that the rate of technological change in our current society makes it impossible to ever completely educate an individual and that the only preparation for life
in an ever-changing society is the preparation to learn continuously
throughout life. Toffler (1970, p. 367) quotes psychologist Herbert
Gerjuoy, of the Human Resources Research Organization, as saying,
"Tomorrow's illiterate will not be the man who can't read; he will
be the man who has not learned how to learn."

Colleges can present several aspects of the need for individual
and community renewal to those who make policy and allocate
funds. First, in humanitarian terms, colleges need to explain and
demonstrate how their programs improve the quality of life in their
communities. In economic terms, the community renewal college
should point out that the difference between being a productive
member of society and being a burden to society lies almost entirely
in education. Finally, in a time when politicians are prone to cite an
"era of limits" as an excuse for inadequate funding, we should not
hesitate to point out the political necessity of lifelong learning. It is
not only the young who vote; in fact, the average age of the elec-
torate is rising. All constituencies in the community elect the people
who secure and allocate funds for education. All constituencies deserve a "piece of the educational pie" to help meet their needs.

Staffing the College

A college dedicated to providing access for development of
the competencies needed by all the diverse members of a changing
community must accept each student at his or her individual level of
educational development and recognize that such a varied constituency can only be reached by a variety of educational delivery
systems. Such a college faces many problems related to staffing that
are very different from those faced and solved routinely by more
traditional institutions. The solution to these problems lies in differentiated staffing, a functional approach that utilizes full-time and
part-time faculty members, paraprofessionals, community volunteers, and peer tutors in meeting student needs. Just as there are no

traditional or nontraditional students in the community renewal college, so must the distinction between traditional and nontraditional faculty be forgotten. The appropriate faculty member for the community renewal college may be a full-time or a part-time employee of the college; he may hold a Ph.D. or no degree; he may be an experienced teacher, a businessman, or a skilled welder—in short, he is appropriate because he is capable of helping a student or group of students develop a needed competency.

Such a diversified approach to meeting the needs of even-more-diverse learners can raise the productivity of education—a condition critical to reducing costs, as pointed out by Drucker (1969, p. 335). Suggesting that teaching today "is where agriculture was around 1750, when it took some twenty men on the farm to feed one nonfarmer in the town," he projects that "by 1999, if present trends . . . continue, half of the population of the United States would be up front teaching with half the population sitting and learning."

The philosophy of the community renewal college demands a staff that accepts and is prepared to implement its basic purposes. All members of such a staff must believe that lifelong learning is an imperative in our changing world; that the college is for everyone and that the elderly citizen interested in a noncredit health-maintenance course or the thirty-year-old laborer interested in developing job skills is as important as the teenaged, full-time, transfer student; that education may occur anywhere—not only on a campus. They must accept the idea that the goals *of* students, translated into competency needs, are more important than predetermined, faculty-set goals *for* students. Above all, they must believe that the college exists for the community and can succeed only so long as it serves the community.

The changing base of community needs upon which the community renewal college is founded requires that the college be flexible—able to respond quickly to a great variety of educational requests. Such flexibility requires that the college be able to assemble people with special skills quickly and for varying periods of time. The community renewal college will, therefore, depend greatly on part-time and temporary staff members for its community programs.

The community renewal college will obtain its instructors

from a variety of sources. Many instructors will be recent graduates of university programs to train teachers or will come from teaching positions at other colleges and universities. A great many, particularly part-time instructors, will come from the community itself. Since the college is usually not their only place of employment, community instructors can be employed for short periods, giving the college the necessary flexibility for community programs. In addition, instructors who come to the college from various segments of the community and maintain their ties and allegiances to the community give the college valuable lines of communication.

The need for continuous staff development will be a particular necessity for the community renewal college. The relationships between the college and its constituencies in the community will be fluid in the sense that the college will adopt the mode of operation most appropriate for a particular group at a particular time. Such a flexible and pluralistic operation will require continual communication within the staff and between staff and administration. The great number of part-time instructors and the resultant turnover will require that attention be given to an ongoing orientation program. Community instructors, many of whom will be teaching for the first time, will need assistance in developing instructional methods and using instructional media, even though they may possess great expertise in their own fields of work. Part-time and off-campus staff members have usually received little attention from the college administration. Because they are such an integral part of the operation of the community renewal college, ways must be found to communicate with them regularly and bring them into the ongoing staff-development program of the college as full partners.

Delivery of Instructional Programs

Regardless of the community orientation of the college's philosophy, the administrative structure, or the carefully selected and trained staff, the truest test of a college's commitment to providing access for the entire community is the extent to which the college is willing to develop innovative, flexible systems that deliver educational programs at times and locations convenient for the students, and through techniques appropriate for the competency being developed and for the students' learning styles. Many students will prefer to come to a campus, will select credit courses leading to a degree, and will choose lecture classes of traditional size and content. The community renewal college will recognize that this most traditional of uses of a college remains valid. However, the college that hopes to attract students other than those who seek out the campus, and wishes to become totally involved in the improvement of the community, must be prepared to move into many types of instructional programs and utilize a wide variety of delivery systems.

For example, Northern Virginia Community College has responded to community needs in its broadly diverse service area by establishing the Extended Learning Institute, which offers credit and noncredit courses on a time- and space-free basis. Students can now take college courses and study at their convenience and at a location of their choosing. Self-paced learning is stressed, so that the student can complete a course when he or she has mastered it. The Extended Learning Institute utilizes several delivery systems, including mass-media-based instruction and course materials designed for individuals to use at home. Courses are developed through close cooperation of faculty members from the five NVCC campuses with instructional technologists and media producers. Students may talk with faculty members by telephone or during personal visits, and may have to come on campus only for a seminar and the final examination.

For centuries the college campus has been a center of learning and teaching. It has also been something of a fortress designed to preserve man's accumulated knowledge. It has been an environment conducive to scholarly pursuits, where students can absorb as much as possible of the wisdom of the ages. This has been an important function of colleges and universities; the campus has preserved our culture through many perilous periods of history. Unfortunately, in providing a place where the few young people most academically inclined can pursue their learning, the university has excluded everyone else. Since providing access to the development of needed competencies for *all* in the community is the purpose of the community renewal college, the college must address itself to the location of community programs. It must ask: How can all the community be attracted to the college? What barriers, physical or psychological, deter learners from seeking competency-developing experiences? What can the college do to overcome these barriers?

For many students the college campus, with its classrooms, lecture halls, laboratories, and learning-resource centers, provides the ideal learning atmosphere. For many others, however, the college campus is not only inconvenient but also uninviting—particularly for people who have not generally found success in academic institutions in the past. These are two very good reasons for taking some college programs off the campus and into the community. A third and equally important reason is that many programs of the community renewal college either cannot or should not be conducted on campus: they require that some part of the community serve as a laboratory, or they at least can be improved if offered in a "real world" laboratory. An example is provided by Hawaii Community College, in Hilo, where classes in cash-register operation are taught in a local supermarket.

The community renewal college will find that it must work with the community to offer programs in every sort of facility imaginable. At present, programs are going on in churches, hospitality rooms of banks, YMCAs, hospitals, nursing homes, restaurants, and municipal facilities, such as parks, pools, auditoriums, concert halls, planetariums, and museums. Programs are being developed in prisons, for the incarcerated, and in plants and businesses, for employees who need on-the-job training. Public and private secondary schools are being used during regular day hours for early-admission programs for high school students, and during after-school hours for community-oriented programs. Some colleges have found that mobile classrooms provide a convenient and effective way to unite college and community.

The educational needs of a small rural population in the state of Washington are being met in a variety of locations by Whatcom Community College. This recently founded college is providing educational services without a campus, using instead such community facilities as churches, offices, high school classrooms, and studios. Whatcom's plan includes a centrally located college service center, which provides supportive administrative services. The key to the success of its development and instructional centers is the community orientation, down to the designation of the person at a desk or phone in his own home as the college contact in that community. Everything from registration, advising, and counseling services to book-buying and secretarial services is delivered where it is needed, providing equal opportunities to all students, wherever they are located in the district.

In addition to the above-stated benefits of using off-campus facilities is the obvious saving to the college and ultimately to the taxpayers. When thousands of students can be served in existing community facilities at little or no cost to the college, the need for costly campus facilities is greatly reduced. This benefit is of real importance to the frequently poorly funded community college, and should be pointed out to governing boards and legislative bodies.

An example of cost efficiency through the use of off-campus facilities is found at San Antonio College, in Texas. A number of years ago the college purchased a service station that had been closed; it is now a piano-tuning school, primarily for blind students drawn from all over the state. This is typical of the way San Antonio College has recycled buildings in its historic city.

Colorado Mountain College found off-campus facilities the solution to the special problems of serving a diverse population thinly scattered over a large rural area.

CASE STUDY: COLORADO MOUNTAIN COLLEGE

Located in the rural, mountainous region of western Colorado, Colorado Mountain College recognized early in its development that the physical characteristics of the land and the dispersion of the population necessitated an innovative, decentralized delivery system. The five counties that form the Colorado Mountain College district extend over an area some 175 miles long and 75 miles wide. There are over twenty communities scattered among the 13,175 square miles of the district. No population center in the district has over 10,000 residents. The total population of the district is estimated at 60,000. Not only is distance a problem in reaching the constituents of this college, the terrain requires the crossing of mountain passes to reach isolated communities.

Aside from the geographical barriers, the breadth of educational needs is staggering. Colorado Mountain College is the only postsecondary institution within the five counties. The communities vary widely, ranging from the affluent resort areas of Aspen, Vail, and Breckenridge to the ranching and mining areas of Rifle, Eagle, Gypsum, Basalt, and Carbondale. Rapid urbanization is affecting the resort communities. In the rural areas, traditional agrarian values are competing with new land-use systems. The populations of Minturn, Redcliff, and Gilman have Chicano majorities. The residents of the district range from rich to poor, highly educated to illiterate, lifelong community residents to new arrivals, sophisticated to provincial.

A community-based approach to delivery of educational services to local populations has been a fundamental success of Colorado Mountain College. The college has clearly demonstrated the viability of its community-based approach through the development of a comprehensive continuing-education program administered through its nine off-campus outreach education centers. These outreach centers have generated a large student enrollment and are continuing to grow at an amazing rate. In 1974, the college's continuing-education program served 11,000 residents. An additional 3,200 students were enrolled on two formal campuses. The growth continued to be dramatic in 1975–1976. Through the first three quarters of the academic year, continuing-education enrollments increased 20 percent over 1974–1975. It is now estimated that the program will serve 15,000 residents in 1975–1976, approximately 25 percent of the total population of the district. Not only has the decentralized approach enabled the college to meet the needs of a widely scattered population, it has allowed the college to provide varied programs to meet the particular needs of the extremely different communities.

Colorado Mountain College is another example of an institution attempting to meet the total educational and renewal needs of its community through a community-based approach. The college is currently experimenting with the use of community access to cable television, contract learning, and adult basic education modeled on the outreach program. A model for an outreach counseling system has been developed and will be implemented as funding is available.

Serving the diverse needs of the community by using locations in the community helps to eliminate one barrier to access. Another equally formidable barrier is the traditional credit-course mode of instruction. Although many competencies can be developed effectively through credit courses (and this book in no way suggests that such courses should be eliminated), many competencies needed in the community simply do not fit into such an arrangement. Noncredit courses and short courses, which are generally more flexible in the amount of time they demand and the kind of competence they develop, are extremely useful alternatives. It must be recognized, however, that many competencies can best be developed through modes other than courses. Institutes, seminars, meetings, workshops, demonstrations, community counseling, and presentations of various sorts are used regularly in many community-oriented colleges. Independent study and autotutorial arrangements make it possible to individualize instruction to a high degree. Co-op educational programs make it possible for students to learn while working in their chosen fields.

For example, at Lone Mountain College, formerly San Francisco College for Women, an unusual community-based approach to career exploration is underway in the Tunbridge Program. The uniqueness of the program stems from several things. Students enrolled in the program include high-school seniors, undergraduates at Lone Mountain, and older adults who wish to explore new career directions or personal interests. Most of its faculty members are off-campus "networkers" practicing in various careers (not professional teachers) who help students experience and learn about those careers. The use of a field faculty, a "network" of people in different occupations to work with students to achieve their educational goals rather than the production goals of the sponsor, helps students ease gradually into the occupational world. The semesters, five months in length, overlap by a month, enabling an incoming student to spend some time with those about to complete the program. After a two-week orientation session in which his interests and goals are carefully studied, the student consults about twenty experts in the area who represent his major fields of interest. He narrows his interests to one or more specific projects and prepares a written "scenario" of the project for his faculty tutor. He spends most of his time during the semester working on the project as contracted for with a community networker and Tunbridge. At least twice a week the student meets on campus with his faculty tutor for group and individual tutorials. He has an exit interview with a faculty/student panel at the end of the term. The option of credit/no-credit or letter grades is available, and the 16 units of credit awarded are often allocated among various academic disciplines. The self-motivated students in the Tunbridge program, assuming the responsibility for their performance, set their own priorities and schedules.

It is important that the college wishing to remove all barriers to lifelong learning understand that not all learning occurs in formal school or college situations. Many students have developed competencies out of school that the college should accept as valid so that the students can gain the necessary credit (if credits and degrees are their goals), meet requirements for further training, or simply receive the same recognition and encouragement given students who develop such competencies in formal programs. Credit by examination, challenge examinations, and CLEP (College Level Educational Preparation) are all designed to assess student learning through prior experience.

The community renewal college will utilize every possible medium to guarantee access to its programs: correspondence study; use of instructional devices, such as computer-assisted, programed, and telephone instruction; directed individual study; tutorials, including private instruction; apprenticeship; internship; classroom instruction; seminars and workshops; laboratory study; assembly, such as lectures and community gatherings; mass-media instruction, including newspaper courses; experiential learning, such as cultural-exchange programs, learning through independent experiences, and do-it-yourself learning; and assessment of prior experiences, as by proficiency and achievement testing, demonstration, and interviewing.

The traditional lecture, whether in a campus classroom or an off-campus facility, will remain an important delivery medium preferred by many students. Many other students, however, learn more effectively in other ways, and the lecture technique is not appropriate for many programs of the community renewal college. Television is a versatile and valuable delivery system. Closed-circuit systems, open-circuit systems, and videotape devices have done much to take education to students. The as yet relatively undeveloped possibilities of cable television and the experimental devices that allow feedback from the student will make this medium even more effective.

Certainly, if the experience of the Open University of the United Kingdom is any guide, there is in all of us the urge to learn. Chartered by the Queen on May 30, 1969, the new university was charged with the responsibility of designing educational approaches to accommodate the life-style of active adults who could study only part-time. In order to tap this reservoir of new students, the Open University made full use of the educational potential of BBC television. In its first five years, it graduated over 4,500 students (170 of whom had no previous college study). Currently, its enrollment is approximately 40,000. It offers sixty-eight interdisciplinary courses in the humanities, social sciences, natural sciences, technology, and mathematics, prepared by academic course teams working cooperatively with BBC producers.

Similar educational experiments have been undertaken by three American institutions—the University of Houston, Rutgers, and the University of Maryland—with encouraging results. Because of the extensive use of televising (in segments) the courses offered, a diversity of students have been able to take advantage of the programs. Most Americans have easy access to TV sets, so that turning the home into a classroom is relatively simple. Betty Jo Mayeske, director of the Open University at the University of Maryland, characterizes that institution's 304 first-year students as follows (1974, pp. 78–79): "The average age of the students is thirty-five years; 63 percent are female, 37 percent male; 17 percent are members of minority groups; 25 percent had no previous college, while 40 percent had not been to school for seven to ten years; 52.63 percent are employed full time, 9.21 percent part time, and 22.3 percent are housewives."

"College by Television" has also been used successfully by two-year colleges. A brochure by that title describes two programs ("Law for the 70's" and "The Consumer Experience") offered by the (San Francisco) Bay Area Community College Television Consortium. It points out that since the consortium was organized, early in 1974, "nearly five thousand residents of the area have enrolled for college credit in the three courses offered thus far, receiving valuable instruction in their homes." Enrollees become duly registered students at their local community colleges, which provide a teacher on each campus who serves as a "guide" for each course and is available for conference either by telephone or in person. This individual also assists students in reviewing the course, and evaluates the midterm and final examinations, which are required of all students.

The City Colleges of Chicago, in addition to their well-known TV College, have initiated "studies unlimited," a new delivery system for their heterogeneous population. TV College offers five or six courses on television every semester; students can watch them at home or in a learning-resources center on campus. In "studies unlimited," a course is placed on a video cassette. Students can come in and register, and then take the course, including the examinations, on their own time.

But perhaps the most significant breakthrough in the field of educational technology is the development of a new system for the transmission of pictures and sound at extremely high speeds. Developed by Goldmark Communication's founder and president, Peter C. Goldmark, who developed the long-playing phonograph record and the first practical color-television system, Rapid Transmission and Storage (RTS) Mark II permits images and sound to be sent by means of regular "over-the-air" broadcasting facilities, by satellite, or by cable television for storage and playback in ordinary television sets in the home or at school.

Six community college districts were scheduled to offer courses over Mark I, an early form of the RTS system, during the fall of 1976, utilizing closed-circuit television in community learning centers, such as libraries, churches, and public schools, in addition to open-circuit television in students' homes. The six college districts, with a total enrollment of more than 200,000 students, are Central Piedmont Community College, of Charlotte, North Carolina; Chicago City Colleges; Coast Community College District, of Costa Mesa, California; the College of DuPage, Illinois; Lane Community College, of Eugene, Oregon; and the Metropolitan Community Colleges, of Kansas City, Missouri. They form the Association of Community Colleges for Excellence in Systems and Services (ACCESS), a consortium formed to develop modular, competency-based courses for delivery over this unique system. The first three courses deal with health sciences, consumer education, and business. Each course will consist of thirty modules (lessons) of about thirty minutes' duration.

The Mark I system can provide sixty half-hour programs from a single hour-long video cassette. Up to thirty of these programs can be selected from the single tape and shown simultaneously on as many sets for multiple-classroom instruction. In addition, Mark I units are portable (small enough to fit in the trunk of a car) and can deliver the desired lessons into learning centers by cable. Thus, several learning centers away from the college campus could offer a number of different lessons from one Mark I unit during any one day. This would allow community colleges to provide a complete course curriculum covering many subjects and accommodating all segments of a community by using a single Mark I unit costing less than $20,000.

The potential of educational radio, eclipsed in its early stages by the glamour of television, should not be overlooked. The great number of radios, their inexpensiveness, and their portability make radio a medium of great value. The production cost of radio programs is only a fraction of that of television programs. When the desired competency can be developed through audio alone, radio is far more cost-efficient and offers access to more people in more places than television.

Audiotape, used either on campus in learning-resource centers or by students in their homes, automobiles, or places of work, is another effective medium. Frequently, the same tapes developed for radio broadcast can be made available for individual students' use. The telephone is only now beginning to be used for instructional purposes. As technology improves, this will be an instrument of great versatility for community instruction. Programed material and computer-assisted instruction will provide opportunities for students to work at their own pace, either on or off campus.

The above is by no means an exhaustive list of instructional media used by the community renewal college in its efforts to remove barriers to access. Our expanding technology will almost daily provide new and exciting means of reaching students with instructional programs. The greater problem for the college will be to find ways of using new media effectively and adapting the other components of the learning situation appropriately.

Many community-based colleges have developed innovative systems of providing access to learning for their constituencies. Through a statewide television and radio consortium in Florida, courses for credit are beamed into the homes of residents of the twenty-eight community college districts. Austin Community College, in Texas, and Wayne County Community College, in Detroit, have merged into their communities, maintaining no formal campuses and taking learning programs to the students. And the University of Mid-America, a consortium of seven universities, utilizes a regional open-learning system of study by radio, television, newspaper, and correspondence to reach thousands of persons of every age in Midwestern and South-Central states. UMA is funded largely by the National Institute of Education, in Washington, D.C. Its member institutions are Iowa State University, Kansas State University, the University of Kansas, the University of Missouri, the University of Nebraska, the University of Oklahoma, and Oklahoma State University.

CASE STUDY: THE COMMUNITY COLLEGE OF VERMONT

Funded by an OEO grant when it was established in 1970, the Community College of Vermont (CCV) has dedicated itself to serving those adults who have no other access to appropriate education. A community-based, competency-based college without a campus, CCV enables Vermonters to continue their education at home, taking courses nearby from instructors who often live in the students' own communities. The college is open to any resident of the state, regardless of age, financial situation, geographic location, or previous educational experience. CCV concentrates its services and efforts especially on people who have been discouraged in the past by high tuition costs, distance from campuses, family or job responsibilities, or limiting admissions policies. At $35 per course, the college has the lowest tuition in the state.

The college provides quality education at reduced cost by

avoiding the duplication of existing services and by using the talent and facilities already available in Vermont's communities. The community is the "campus": classes are held in local schools, offices, banks, factories, churches—wherever communities have donated space for ccv's use. A class in auto mechanics may meet at a service station, a creative-writing class in a public library, and a psychology class in a local church.

Instructors are also drawn from the general community. Paid on a per-course basis, they usually hold full-time jobs in the community, practicing the skills they teach. A certified public accountant may teach accounting, an architect may instruct students in mechanical drawing, a town official may conduct a workshop in local government, the director of a day-care center may supervise on-the-job training for a ccv student. The community college, in selecting competent teachers, values demonstrated knowledge in a field as much as formal education.

The ccv staff operates out of one central administrative office and nine field offices located throughout the state. Many outreach activities are directed from each of these field offices, thereby carrying learning opportunities and materials even further into Vermont's rural communities. The staff talks enthusiastically of "taking learning experiences to students instead of making students come to college." As might be expected, recruiting students is a nonexistent activity at ccv. Time, effort, and funds are spent, instead, on *outreach*— literally, reaching out to take services and resources to Vermont's adults as they continue to work and live in their own communities. Not just "community-based," the college might almost be said to be "community-placed."

Full-time staff members at the college do not teach, in the traditional sense of the term. Other than the fifteen or so individuals who make up the administration, ccv's staff members spend their time and energy on counseling students or guiding instructors. The members of the instructor-support staff, known as "coordinators of instruction," have three major responsibilities: through the use of questionnaires and contact with the community, they determine the community's needs for learning; by meeting and talking with community leaders, merchants, churchmen, and so forth, they secure space and facilities for college use; and, in interviews and discussions, they orient instructors and prospective instructors to the community college philosophy, give them instructional guidance and media support, and generally provide them with a person to turn to at any point during their teaching experience with the nontraditional college.

Counselors, referred to collectively as "student support," make up the greater portion of the full-time field staff. Whereas there may be only one or two coordinators of instruction for each region in which the college operates, counselors work out of each of the nine field offices. As the title of their division of the staff implies, they support students by providing advice, counseling, and direction. Rather than teaching *content,* these ccv staff members are dedicated to teaching the *process* of learning.

ccv students receive neither grades nor credits. Instead, the two-year associate degree is awarded on the basis of demonstrated skills and the acquisition of competencies agreed upon in advance. Each student desiring a degree meets regularly with a ccv counselor to draw up a "contract," which defines the student's goals in a chosen area of study. It is this process of "contracting" that forms the bulwark of ccv's commitment to learning. Past work experience can be evaluated and included in a study plan. Learning outside the classroom is encouraged. On-the-job training, apprenticeships, and independent study are important in many ccv students' learning programs. At the end of each course or learning experience, the student writes a narrative evaluation of his own performance and the value to him of the course. On the same evaluation form, the instructor writes an evaluation of the student's progress and areas for improvement.

In addition to self-evaluation, evaluation by instructors, and consultation with counselors, each degree candidate meets periodically with a "local review committee." This advisory and evaluative group comprises a fellow student, a ccv staff member, a community instructor, and an additional community member chosen by the student. At regular intervals, the student meets with the review committee to evaluate progress toward the degree.

Three programs of study, each with its own set of competencies, lead to an associate degree: Administrative Services, a program of study for students seeking office- or business-management skills; Human Services, for those interested in counseling, teaching, or related professions; and General Studies, for students interested in other areas. The local review committee considers a program of study completed when the student can demonstrate the acquisition of the competencies and skills specified in the program.

A great number of ccv students enroll for a course or two each term and continue taking courses on a sporadic, nonprogramed basis, depending on the time and money left available by family and job responsibilities. The average ccv student is fully employed during the day, has a family and a low income, and first enrolls in a ccv evening or weekend course to improve job skills, to acquire a craft or hobby, or just "to get out of the house." The college offers a wide range of courses in crafts, physical recreation, and home arts. Offerings in printing, auto mechanics, home plumbing, and yoga are perennially popular. When students do require credits for transfer to other institutions, the college uses the guidelines of the Carnegie Unit to arrive at semester-hour equivalent credits, depending on the amount of time spent in class.

ccv provides different types of students with a variety of instructional settings. Classes, independent study, experiential learning, and on-the-job training are all options made available to a diversity of learners. A fifth instructional model is the Cluster, a support group of students who meet together regularly to discuss with others their own problems, goals, hopes, and fears. This model is seen as most effective for those students who would be reluctant, for a variety of personal and educational reasons, to pursue their own education without peer support. Gradually, these students become more independently involved in courses and other learning experiences, but they return periodically to the Cluster for support and feedback.

The Community College of Vermont has gone to great lengths in its first five years to make learning a lifelong resource for Vermont's people. In December 1975, its nontraditional, noncampus, community- and competency-based system received full accreditation by the New England Association of Schools and Colleges, Inc. A member of the state colleges system since 1972, the college now enables the state to deliver fully accredited, postsecondary education to adults who otherwise would have no access to it. The flexibility and variety of its instructional models, planning, management, and budgeting are all effectively bringing learners together with resources.

V

Making Programs
Individualized and
Competency-Based

To those who cared to look, it was discernible in the mid-fifties: change was on its way—rapid change that was profoundly to affect education, particularly postsecondary education, by the mid-seventies. The "systems approach" to management was becoming a major preoccupation in business and industry. Manufacturers, encouraged by the success of the computer, were beginning to experiment with new forms of technological equipment. The behavioral scientists, after years of struggle for recognition, were making their voices heard: though "behavioral change" probably was only vaguely understood by the layman, academicians were beginning to consider its application to the business of learning. And colleges—particularly community colleges—were sprouting across the land at the rate of approximately one every ten days. Everything augured well for the "universal higher education" the President's Commission on Higher Education had promised in 1947.

During the sixties, the "in" word in education was *relevance*. Nobody quite knew what it meant, because nobody was able to define it precisely. No satisfactory answer was forthcoming to the question, "Relevance for what?" As a result, it became a word out of context, bruited about with resounding vehemence, but virtually without meaning in the end. Students, growing dissatisfied with the education they were receiving, began to rebel against the collegiate status quo and began to clamor for "relevance." Parents, too, were in revolt. "What's wrong?" they complained. "Our kids aren't learning anything in school."

Then, in the opening years of the seventies, from every part of the nation, the call for accountability was heard. Educational administrators and boards of trustees were quick to respond with policies on accountability; educational-consulting firms sprang opportunistically into being and teamed with manufacturers of learning aids, "guaranteeing" learning through use of their inventions (which, though not altogether successful, did give the education industry a jolt); and higher education—at least the community college segment of it—adapted the systems approach from business and industry to solve quantifiable problems of the teaching/learning process.

Now, in the mid-seventies, educators concerned about developing *performance-oriented* as well as community-based programs are embracing "competency" as if that were a new concept in education. It is not. Competency is the purpose of education and has been ever since Socrates walked "leisurely through the agora, undisturbed by the bedlam of politics, buttonholing his prey, gathering the young and learned about him, luring them into some shady nook of the temple porticos, and asking them to define their terms" (Durant, 1926, p. 5).

As Roueche, Herrscher, and Baker point out (1976, p. 5), there are many similarities between competency-based education and the traditional means of certifying individuals as competent: "Segments of higher education have attempted competency-based in-

struction in the past. Law school graduates must pass bar examinations. Engineers must score at a preselected level on qualifying
examinations to be authorized to practice in a given state. Nurses are
required to pass state board exams. Only recently, however, have we
begun to look for the tools to certify the competence, at some level, of
the graduates of career programs, parallel college-transfer programs,
and developmental programs." They further conclude that competency-based instruction's intent now is to ensure mastery of a given
program as well.

Competency, as a matter of fact, is a requirement for survival
in the last quarter of the twentieth century. Integrity in the educational system demands that teachers help their students to learn
competencies and that students be able to use the competencies thus
acquired to benefit them in later life. It is fitting that the community
renewal college should be one of the pioneers in implementing this
concept. Espousing the belief that the ability to learn is not limited
to the academically ambitious, community-based colleges have open-
door admissions policies that welcome, besides the high school graduate, any person who can profit from the programs offered.

Nevertheless, an incontrovertible fact is that many community-based colleges have held too idealistic a view of their mission,
being satisfied that they were fulfilling it by merely making educational
opportunities available to students whom the most selective four-year
institutions would leave untouched. In most instances, however,
they have adhered slavishly to the same kinds of instruction so deeply
entrenched in the traditional four-year colleges and universities that
have barred those aspiring students. As a result, many educators have
become convinced that only a small percentage of the "new students" have the capacity to learn what is being taught.

In some respects, this may be true, for *what is being taught* is
not always synonymous with *what can be learned*. Though educators
have talked for years about "individual differences" among learners,
few, until recently, have made any serious attempts to relate those
differences to varying strategies that promote learning. In such circumstances, the colleges have not been conspicuously successful in
implementing the concept of the open door. Contrary to their
idealistic purposes, they have merely multiplied students' frustrations
until the slower ones have become discouraged and either dropped

out or flunked out. After-college performance competency was left almost exclusively to the graduates' own ability to apply the fragments of knowledge they were able to retrieve. The current emphasis on performance-oriented and competency-based education has significance for students in all colleges, both traditional and nontraditional.

In the community renewal college, the content of what will be taught is determined by the particular needs of the community, and it is organized into modules, or units. Required competencies are defined in performance terms for all units, courses, and programs. The concepts of social promotion and social graduation are rejected, along with the conventional grading system, which, all too frequently, produces a "B— automotive mechanic"—that is, an auto mechanic who received an A for the unit in taking the engine apart and a D for the unit in putting it back together, for a final course, grade of B—. The performance orientation of all programs offered by the community renewal college requires that *all* competencies be mastered.

An excellent example of a competency-based, performance-oriented program is offered by Florida Junior College at Jacksonville. Although probably not high on any community's scale of pressing societal needs, aviation landing is a clear example of a community need with a strong performance orientation for which a course was developed. Called "Pinch Hitter," the course is not a course in flight technology, not a course that prepares the student to become licensed to fly, but a course that prepares the small-aircraft passenger to control and land a plane in an emergency, in case anything happens to the pilot. Being able to do that is a felt need, and it originated in the community the college serves.

Almost all students who go to college take with them the hope that they will succeed. In the traditional four-year institution, fulfillment of that hope rests almost entirely upon the student's ability to negotiate specified academic hurdles within specified time limits. In the community renewal college, such a system cannot prevail if the college is to live up to its promise to help all students become all that they are capable of becoming. Whether or not students aspire to a bachelor's degree, they can make significant contributions to their society if the college provides them with the necessary social and competency-based skills. What really counts is the kind of persons the college develops: what they can do, how well they can live and work with others, what they can contribute to those others.

Individualized Learning

Although most community colleges today are facing new demands from new students, many are still attempting to meet these demands in the same old shopworn ways. Educators sometimes get caught up in their own rhetoric, seeming to forget that individual differences exist and that what causes one student to learn falls far short for another. They continue to base their educational programs on the "black-coffee syndrome," that peculiar phenomenon exemplified in most student-union vending machines. These offer students the choice of black coffee, coffee with sugar, coffee with cream, coffee with sugar and cream, coffee with two lumps of sugar, coffee with double cream, and so forth; yet the machines deliver only black coffee. Evidently, many colleges fail to recognize the fact of human diversity. This conclusion is perhaps best illustrated by the Fable of the Animal School (source unknown):

Once upon a time, the animals decided they must do something heroic to meet the problems of "a new world," so they organized a school. They adopted an activity curriculum consisting of running, climbing, swimming, and flying. To make it easier to administer, all the animals took all the subjects.

The Duck was excellent in swimming (better, in fact, than her instructor), and made passing grades in flying, but she was very poor in running. Since she was slow in running, she had to stay after school and also drop swimming to practice running. This was kept up until her webbed feet were badly worn and she was only average in swimming. But average was acceptable in school, so nobody worried about that except the Duck.

The Rabbit started at the top of the class in running, but had a nervous breakdown because of so much makeup work in swimming. The Squirrel was excellent in climbing, until he developed frustration in the flying class because his teacher made him start from the ground up instead of from the treetop down. He also developed charley horses from overexertion, and then got C in climbing and D in running.

The Eagle was a problem child and was disciplined severely. In the climbing class he beat all the others to the top of the tree, but insisted on using his own way to get there.

At the end of the year, an abnormal Eel that could swim exceedingly well and also run, climb, and fly a little had the highest average and was valedictorian.

The Prairie Dogs stayed out of school and fought the tax levy because the administration would not add digging and burrowing to the curriculum. They apprenticed their child to a Badger and later joined the Groundhogs and Gophers to start a successful private school.

People are different, and any attempt to fashion all in the same mold rather than capitalize on individual strengths and potentialities results in overall mediocrity. Individual talents go unrecognized, untapped, and undeveloped. Cross has studied extensively the "new student" and has reported her findings in depth in her books (1971, 1976) and speeches. In summary, she has found that widespread reliance on academic-aptitude tests has created a bias against those who test low in academic aptitude, who are female, or who have minority ethnic status; educators have focused on making "new students" over in the image of traditional students through remedial and compensatory programs; traditional college programs are not prepared to handle the learning needs of "new students"; and these students require teaching methods that will support a positive self-concept, will take advantage of their cognitive strengths, and will include interest in and friendliness toward them. Therefore, in the community renewal college an effort is made not only to recognize individual differences among students but to provide instructional strategies that accommodate the variety of learning styles reflected in those differences. (Cross points [1976, p. 54] out that "the goal of all advocates of individualized instruction is to present instructional materials in a way that is maximally useful to the individual.") Such an eclectic approach, while utilizing technological learning aids to their fullest advantage, embraces traditional modes of instruction as well.

First, there must be agreement on a philosophy of education which essentially avows that everyone can learn what he needs to know; that capacity to learn is limited only by the time required to master learning tasks; that an in-depth analysis of what must and can be learned produces better learning materials; that organizing learners in new ways removes many stumbling blocks to learning inherent in traditional strategies and modes; and that effective evaluation provides information on how well the student is progressing.

Second, agreement must be reached on the adoption of learning systems that embrace many of the nontraditional concepts which began to surface two decades ago and which, by the early sixties, were beginning to challenge conventional teaching/learning theories. As Gardner (1964, p. 12) pointed out at that time, "The ultimate goal of the educational system is to shift to the individual the burden of pursuing his own education. This will not be a widely shared pursuit until we get over our odd conviction that education is what goes on in school buildings and nowhere else . . . The world is an incomparable classroom, and life is a memorable teacher for those who are not afraid of her."

Because nontraditionalism is more a feature of methodology than of content, it can serve student bodies who are not exclusively of "college age," as well as those who are. Fundamentally, the nontraditional stance advocates that the student assume responsibility for his own education; that his learning activities be directed toward acquiring competencies instead of merely accumulating credits; and that his personal development be unrestricted by traditional time limitations. But it also provides for competent teacher supervision of each student's activities in the process of acquiring his education. In recognizing that many community members can be as effective in teaching as credentialed individuals, it accepts and attempts to implement that dimension of learning advocated by Mead (1959): "the *lateral* transmission to every sentient member of society, of what has just been discovered, invented, created, manufactured, or marketed . . . a sharing of knowledge by the informed with the uninformed" (p. 16).

In short, nontraditional education can be said to emulate in some degree the hospital model, characterized by diagnosis, prescription, and treatment; in place of illnesses, nontraditional education treats human needs. The past distinction between hospitals and educational institutions has been that hospitals did prescribe different treatment for different patients, while colleges gave each student the same lecture/textbook "treatment," regardless of individual needs, explaining treatment failures largely on the basis of the students' inadequacies. This is tantamount to the hospital's saying, "There's nothing wrong with the treatment; we just keep getting the wrong patients." The sad truth is that, though doctors, as the cliche goes, may be able to bury their "mistakes," educators have to co-exist with theirs for the rest of their lives. Probably the best-kept secret of the academic world is that institutions' reputations tell us more about admissions policies than about teaching proficiencies. Again like the hospital, the community renewal college designs its programs on a "drop in/drop out" basis, providing short- or long-term therapy as diagnosis indicates. This implies a new role for the teacher, the role of learning manager—one who plans for each student strategies that will cause him to learn.

Ideally, individualized learning requires the teacher to work on a one-to-one basis with the student, in what is, essentially, a tutorial program. Such a program, of course, is unworkable in colleges designed to accommodate several thousand students. One partial solution is differentiated staffing. Another is educational technology, which can provide individualized learning for all students as well as increase the productivity of the professional staff. The process of introducing technology requires investment in both hard- and software. But we must recognize that cramming facts into students' heads does little, if anything, to advance the cause of education—namely, to produce a maximum number of self-confident, self-motivating, self-reliant citizens for active participation in American life. Furthermore, the current knowledge explosion, in which the total of man's factual knowledge doubles every ten years, makes it impossible to hire enough teachers who know and can disseminate this larger body of factual knowledge to students. Differentiated staffing and judicious use of educational technology provide useful answers to the question how best to meet the needs of the greatest number of students. But they do not provide the only answers. For students who can function as well within a group framework as in a one-to-one situation, individual curricular programs can be developed according to each student's learning prescription, based on individual and group diagnostic testing.

Stated simply, then, individualized learning stipulates

1. That required competencies (learning objectives) are defined in advance for all units, courses, and programs on the
   basis of a task analysis of requirements for job entry, upper-
   division transfer, and general education.
2. That course and program competencies must be mastered if
   credit is to be given and a degree awarded.
3. That a wide diversity of learning modes and strategies are
   used. Students can learn through their eyes, through their
   ears, or with their hands. Students in the same course might
   receive the material in different ways—from a lecture, from
   a film strip, by building a model, or all three.
4. That all learning experiences must be evaluated, using different techniques, to determine whether the desired learning
   has occurred.
5. That the learning rate must be adjusted to the needs of
   individual students, taking into account the amount of time
   required by the learner to master learning tasks (self-pacing).
6. That the student must assume responsibility for his learning.

Competency-Based Learning Systems

The foregoing principles of individualized learning were
utilized by Brookdale Community College, in New Jersey, in developing competency-based learning systems that featured five major
components. The first of these is the individualized learning prescription based on diagnosis of the student's needs and drawn up by
his counselor. If the student needs no remediation and is ready to
embark upon college-level study, he will be required to take one unit
at a time and remain in that unit until he has achieved a specified
level of competency. This may require a variety of teaching methods
until impartial evaluation reveals that the student understands the
concept covered by the unit or has mastered the skill to which it
applies. Because the criteria for such attainment have been couched
in behavioral terms, it is easy enough to determine whether full
mastery of the unit has been achieved.

This procedure will be particularly valuable in meeting the
needs of the nontraditional students who are coming to the com-

munity college, and will continue to come in increasing numbers as skills acquired earlier become obsolete in a society growing more technological day by day. For whatever reasons, these students usually have been away from school for a long time and need the encouragement that experiencing success, even unit by unit, can give them. Moreover, some of them remember former unhappy experiences under the traditional practice of the teacher's evaluating achievement from high to low within a class, frequently using as criteria the achievements of the most-able students. As a result of that practice, many students performed at a level below standards acceptable to the teacher, and some failed. Therefore, a second component of competency-based learning is adjustment of the learning pace to the needs of the individual student, providing for varying amounts of time to attain the stipulated competencies. This does not mean that standards are lowered; it means only that individual differences in learning rates are recognized and allowance is made for them.

Allowing students to proceed at varying rates, however, requires frequent evaluation of each student's progress to determine whether the desired learning is taking place. Obviously, this cannot be done by scheduling a quiz on a given unit for an entire class, as done traditionally. This impossibility leads to the third component of competency-based learning. Along with course objectives, the teacher develops both comprehensive and diagnostic tests for evaluating each unit—the first to determine degree of mastery and the second to discover areas in which the student is still weak. The test scoring, record keeping, and the like that frequent evaluations of each student require could weigh heavily upon the teacher's time. With differentiated staffing and the professional-team approach, however, the teacher can rely for assistance upon the paraprofessional or clerk assigned to the team, thus being freed for more important tasks.

Under these conditions the teacher's role changes from disseminator of information to manager of learning—the fourth component. What does it mean to be a manager of learning? In this new role, the teacher assumes the important task of creatively inducing student learning. And, to assist the teacher in this transition, the team leader, working cooperatively with other team members, takes the lead in planning each student's program according to that student's learning prescription, in selecting a variety of learning packages, in working with students individually or in small groups, and in monitoring student progress.

As a result of these combined efforts, most students can find the path to learning best suited to their own learning styles, and can realize that learning is an adventure that grows more exciting as they pursue it throughout life. Accordingly, the fifth component of the learning system posits that, with the machinery for learning embodied in the first four now in motion, students will assume more responsibility for their intellectual and personal development, taking an active rather than a passive role. Because numerous technological aids are available to present the facts necessary to a foundational knowledge in a given subject, the student is stimulated to explore tangential avenues of his own, relying on the teacher for help only when some detail baffles him. In the process, he learns not only course material but how to learn and how to help others learn.

We have hypothesized that individualized instruction lets almost every student become a teacher part of the time. We base this hypothesis on the observation that when the student teaches he learns better how to express himself in terms that are easily understood and to recognize both good and poor study habits. At one college, when students were asked to identify the individuals on campus who had been of most help to them, a very large number indicated "other students." It was assumed that so-called "slow" students might hesitate to reveal to their instructors their lagging ability to grasp a skill or concept, but might be less hesitant about admitting it to their peers; this was found to be true. It was also assumed that a majority of such students would seek the help of those they considered "bright" students in overcoming their difficulties. Surprisingly, this was not so. Instead, they had gravitated toward students who had formerly had learning problems similar to their own but who had finally overcome those problems.

Inherent in an instructional system of the type suggested above, of course, are several basic requirements. First, the teachers must be committed to the inducement of students to learn, to the development of their own skills in designing courses that enhance the total curricular pattern, and to the delivery of these courses to students by whatever modes will result in maximum learning. Second, course goals must be specified. The specifications must include the necessary student behavior to show mastery and the conditions under which this behavior will be performed, as well as minimum performance criteria. Third, the notion of student failure must be minimized.

All of this implies allowance for self-paced learning, and the removal of specified time limits within which students must complete all objectives. Designed primarily for the slow learner, self-paced learning nevertheless also benefits the rapid learner. Although most students eventually master learning tasks, some master them much more rapidly than others. Hence, from the outset it is the responsibility of the teacher to discover the amount of time each student needs to master the learning experiences that produce the competency to be acquired in the course of study.

Many traditional as well as nontraditional learners entering college have not established educational or lifetime goals; consequently, these learners may wander from course to course and discipline to discipline until they graduate or drop out. Such a situation is not a characteristic of a competency-based learning system.

A competency-based learning system may be defined as a system that prepares its students to be lifelong learners by helping them determine "where they are" and "where they want to go," by guiding them in setting goals, by helping them establish a commitment to accomplish those goals, by providing them with learning tools that help them do so, by helping them verify their attainment of competencies, by placing them, according to their competencies, in locations where they will be productive members of the community, and by revising the system as a result of input from the learners and other interested members of the community.

Furthermore, a competency-based learning system embraces at least five aims of instruction that leading reform spokesmen (Bruner, 1960; Gardner, 1961; Goodlad and others, 1966; Heathers, 1961; Henry, 1962) have repeatedly been emphasizing: (1) Teach the structure of a discipline, rather than just the facts, by focusing upon the general principles that enable one to explain or predict phenomena in that discipline. (2) Teach the methods of inquiry or problem-solving thinking that are employed in the discipline. (3)

Teach competencies in independent study so that students become capable of planning and conducting their own learning activities. (4) Set standards of excellence for mastery, holding all students to whatever levels of accomplishment correspond to those standards, and suit the learning task, methods of instruction, and rate of advancement to the student's learning characteristics. (5) Individualize instruction through programs of studies tailored to a student's needs and capabilities.

Implementation of a learning system that embodies these principles and others suggested in the foregoing pages will do much, as Gardner (1964, p. 21) suggests, "to develop skills, attitudes, habits of mind, and the kinds of knowledge and understanding that will be the instruments of continuous change and growth on the part of the [student]. Then we will have fashioned *a system that provides for its own continuous renewal.*"

The sixties and the seventies were replete with examples of attempts by countless educational institutions to attract more students, produce greater learning results, and provide more ways to reach the individual than had ever been accomplished through traditional approaches. These included the early development and utilization of the autotutorial approach, as at Purdue University, in Indiana, and Oakland and Lansing Community Colleges, in Michigan; efforts, as by Lane Community College, in Oregon, and College of the Mainland, in Texas, to provide instructional strategies that would accommodate the variety of learning styles among students; and the development of learning systems based on performance objectives, as at El Paso Community College, in Texas, and Burlington County College, in New Jersey. All these approaches required that learning objectives (competencies) be defined in measurable terms for all units, courses, and programs and that all competencies be mastered if credit was to be given or a degree awarded.

CASE STUDY: PIONEER COMMUNITY COLLEGE

Pioneer Community College, one of Kansas City's four Metropolitan Community Colleges, has one of the largest "campuses" in the nation, encompassing the counties of Cass, Clay, Jackson, and Platte, Missouri, an area with approximately one million persons. Utilizing storefronts, factories, offices, homes, apartments, and five branches of the city's library system, Pioneer, a community-based, performance-oriented college, is one of the most unusual two-year colleges in America. Aside from the fact that it has no "brick and mortar" campus, no set curriculum, and few full-time teachers, it has adopted a revolutionary philosophy—a philosophy that places the individual and his educational needs and goals ahead of a rigidly defined curriculum, recognizing that more is required than outreach to constitute community-based education.

Pioneer evolved from the Metropolitan Institute of Community Services, begun in 1974 for the purpose of expanding and coordinating services throughout the community college district so that all citizens might have an opportunity to enhance and enrich their lives. Instead of offering to the community a series of predetermined educational experiences, the institute found out from the learners themselves what they actually wanted and needed. Some 24,000 citizens took advantage of the opportunity to make their wishes known during the first year and a half. William Keim, Pioneer's first president, directed the assessment study, which led to the identification of groups of nontraditional clientele who were not being adequately served by the existing three conventional community colleges in the Metropolitan system. Among these clients were the aged; the underchallenged woman; the handicapped; the under- and unemployed; those with access problems; the motivationally disadvantaged; and those with special needs, such as those whose jobs require updated or extended skills. Since these groups are traditionally the hardest to reach, special effort was made to plan an administrative structure that would encourage their recruitment and orientation. The college uses varied teaching tools, such as television, cassettes, learning machines, and computers, to accommodate these different kinds of learners.

Pioneer is developing an individualized, self-paced, continuous-progress learning system in which the student, the counselor, and an adviser in the student's elected field decide how the student is to go about achieving, on a contract basis, the competencies he or she has selected. The point is to prepare students with what they need to

know through a student-centered experience rather than to have
them meet the arbitrary requirements of a formal degree-oriented
system.

Since the four Metropolitan Community Colleges see themselves as partners in the development of the ten-year master plan that
led to Pioneer, there is constant sharing and communication between
the three more-traditional colleges with campuses and the new noncampus college. For example, faculty members are shared, thereby
increasing the use of nontraditional methods at the three original
colleges while reaping at Pioneer the benefits of experience and excellence in teaching. Faculty members from the three original colleges also serve on curriculum task forces to define program competencies and develop instructional materials.

Recognizing that community-based education requires nontraditional approaches, Pioneer bases its structure on the following
flow process:

Identification
↓
Diagnosis
↓
Prescription
↓
Treatment
↓
Evaluation

Pioneer's educational philosophy is founded on the needs of ordinary
Americans: personal development, human interaction, marketable
skills, and citizen responsibilities.

Pioneer's modularized, competency-based system (not yet
fully developed or implemented) is based on the definition of a
competency-based learning system given earlier in this chapter. Below we present a model developed from that definition—the model
that Pioneer will follow.

The *orientation* process is the most crucial component in a
competency-based learning system. This component addresses the
learner's questions "Where am I?" and "Where do I want to go?"

It is primary in preparing learners to pursue learning interests throughout life.

The orientation process may vary from individual to individual, and for a single individual it may vary from one learning commitment to another. However, the process, in a competency-based learning system, should be continual for each learner.

The orientation process must allow for individual differences, and hence it must consist of units of activity that encompass some or all learning experiences in self-awareness, decision-making, career exploration, learning styles, learning processes, assessment of one's knowledge and skills gained through previous education experiences or on-the-job experiences, and setting of goals (for one's life as well as for one's education). Upon completion of this phase of the orientation, the learner should be aware of his or her present competencies and be able to establish goals that will enable him or her to be a greater asset to the community.

An integral part of the ongoing orientation process is the learner interaction group. Such a group has two purposes: it provides emotional support, and it allows the learner's peers to impart information about their competencies. Another part of the ongoing orientation is a communication system that will continually inform learners about what is happening at the college and in the community, be it operational or general information. There is at least one other part in the ongoing orientation that must be included, that is the learner follow-up. Follow-up sessions provide the learner with a chance to reflect on his or her goals and reevaluate their worth.

In general, the members of the counseling staff are responsible for learner orientation. They are sharing the ongoing orientation activities with the instructors and administrators and also are providing the leadership necessary to ensure viable orientation activities.

Once the learner has set a goal, the next step in the system is to develop the *competency objectives.* The learner, with the aid of a counselor, reviews the prescribed competencies relating to the accomplishment of his or her goal(s). These competencies are established by the college, professionals in the learner's field or career area, curriculum advisers, or a combination thereof. Once the prescribed competencies have been reviewed, a study of those competencies believed to be possessed by the learner is made, and the two sets of competencies are compared. Any prescribed competencies that the learner has already attained are then documented. (Documentation is the process of ascertaining that the learner in fact possesses the competency in a degree equal to or greater than that prescribed.) Then the learner and counselor begin the task of developing competency objectives for the remaining (undocumented) competencies. The competency objectives normally are broad in scope and the predicted outcomes general in nature. A competency objective identifies (1) the kind of ability that the learner must exhibit, (2) the level of performance, (3) the time by which the learner must have achieved that competency, and (4) the method of verifying the competency.

After the objectives have been stated, the learner selects at least two but no more than four persons to sit with his or her counselor on a panel. Members joining the counselor on the panel will be selected from the faculty and from people in the community with expertise in the area of the learner's specialty. The sole purpose of this panel is to advise the learner while he or she is partaking of learning experiences in the college. The activities of the panel are (1) reviewing the learner's competency-based objectives, (2) developing a learning plan of action, (3) designing a learning agreement, and (4) reviewing the learner's evaluation of the system.

When the panel has been selected, its members are given the list of competency-based objectives and the list of documented competencies. After reviewing the competency objectives, the panel develops the learning plan of action. The learning plan of action prescribes those learning experiences that must be completed before the learner can accomplish his or her stated objectives. When the panel finishes the plan of action, the counselor carefully reviews it with the learner. A learner who believes he or she has a competency, not previously identified, for which learning is prescribed in the plan of action, may challenge that prescription. If the challenge is successful, the learning experience will be deleted from the plan of action. Following the learner's review, the plan is confirmed and lodged with the panel.

Next, the advisory panel draws up a *learning agreement*, which contains the objectives, the documented competencies, the learning plan of action, the review plan (which is developed from the objectives and which identifies method of review of objectives, time between reviews, and reviewers), and the statement of default.

When the learning agreement is completed, the advisory panel and the learner meet to discuss and sign the agreement. The agreement is discussed in detail and all parties are given an opportunity to question or challenge any part of it. The statement of default, which describes the courses of action open to the learner or the college should either party not meet the commitments specified in the agreement, is the final section of the agreement and is carefully reviewed for possible inconsistencies. With the review of the agreement completed, each member of the panel and the learner sign the learning agreement. Copies of the agreement are given to each member of the panel and to the learner; one copy goes into the college's file. The panel may, at this point, dissolve; however, the learner may continue to seek advice from any or all members of the panel as necessary.

The learning experiences prescribed in the learning plan of action may include core courses, long or short courses, and on-the-job training. All content materials are of modular design, and these modules are the *learning tools* in the system. The learning tools are defined as those elements in a learning system which impart knowledge and enhance skills. The learning tools (modules) are self-contained where possible, and are composed of the following components. (These components make up a system of instruction tested between 1969 and 1972 by the staff of the Junior Community College Division of the National Laboratory for Higher Education, Durham, North Carolina.)

> The *rationale* explains why it is important (or relevant) for the learner to achieve the objectives. The learner must recognize *why* it is important that he or she master the knowledge or skills dealt with in the module.

> *Performance objectives* specify, in a measurable form, criteria for evaluating the learner's performance.

> A *pretest* of the learner's capability precedes formal instruction. The pretest, based upon the objectives of the module, helps to determine (1) whether the learner has the prerequisite skills or knowledge to be able to profit from the instruction; (2)

whether the learner has mastered some or all of the performance objectives; and (3) where the learner should be placed in the sequence of learning activities.

Learning activities are means to an end, not ends in themselves. A learning activity is made up of three parts: input, practice, and demonstration of the learning acquired. Learning activities may be programed from the specific to the general or reverse, using various forms of media.

The *posttest* is a vital element in the learning module. It is designed to measure the attainment of the performance objective.

The final component is *revision*. An aid in revision is a data sheet designed to determine where learners had difficulty in the instructional process and to identify the learners' attitudes toward the learning activities.

Most modules are developed by the faculty, but faculty members are encouraged to use off-the-shelf materials (with or without modification) if the materials are appropriate.

When the learner completes all of the learning experiences prescribed in the learning plan, he or she will have mastered the performance objectives for each module included in that learning experience. When all learning experiences have been accomplished for a given objective, the learner is then ready to validate his or her level of competency.

The *objectives review* is the process by which a learner verifies that the competencies stated in his or her objectives have been accomplished at the desired level of proficiency. The method of verification of the competencies is described in the objective(s) and is carried out when the learner has completed all the learning experiences prescribed in the learning plan to accomplish that objective.

If the competencies are verified, the learner continues following the learning plan of action as described in the agreement. If the competencies are not verified, then the plan of action must be modified and a new set of learning experiences prescribed to overcome the deficiencies.

Each competency specified in the learning agreement is reviewed in accordance with the method stated in the agreement. When all competencies in all objectives have been attained, the learning agreement becomes dormant. A learner may rejuvenate the learning agreement at any time. Additional objectives and other information then form an addendum to the original learning agreement.

The *placement* of learners may be a key element in the competency-based learning system. The college should be able to provide locations in the community where learners can apply for job placement. This effort provides a good opportunity for members of the community to become involved in the operations of the college. Learners may be placed in jobs in the community for on-the-job learning experiences. An employer may specify what competencies will be required of his or her employees in years to come, and, if the college agrees to train people accordingly, may guarantee job placement to learners during their beginning learning experiences. Extensive college/community interaction for the purpose of developing the competencies of the learners to meet the needs of businesses would merge the college with the community.

System evaluation occurs after the learning agreement has become dormant. The learner is asked to evaluate the competency-based learning system in general and the learning plan of action in detail.

The general evaluation reveals attitudes generated as a result of going through the system. Learners' responses are collected and compiled to provide a data base for revising the system.

The evaluation of the learning plan of action is based on the learner's expected outcomes, relevance to accomplishing the required competencies, appropriateness of the learning strategies, compatibility of learning experiences and learning styles, availability of advisers and instructional specialists for communication, and impressions of interaction groups.

When the learner completes the evaluation, the raw data are given to the learner's advisory panel. The panel prepares a report of the data generated and sends it to the appropriate college official. A follow-up evaluation, similar to the original evaluation, is conducted two to five years after the learner has been placed in a job. In addition, each employer is periodically asked to evaluate the competencies of employees who were previously learners in the college.

VI

Ensuring Institutional
Self-Renewal

◆◆

The major thesis of this book is the
sharply increased need for continual renewal of individuals, institutions, and the total community in a time of rapid social, cultural,
and technological change. The alternatives to renewal, we believe,
are frustration, stultification, and disorientation of the individual;
stagnation and eventual disintegration of community institutions;
and, ultimately, decay of the community itself. Fortunately, individuals and institutions are beginning to discover the need for renewal and are seeking help by availing themselves of opportunities
for personal and institutional development. Some American colleges
have played an active role in this awakening on the part of individuals and institutions. Others are only now beginning to recognize
the need to organize for individual and community renewal.

Even those community-based colleges most concerned with

114

renewal, however, have been concerned more with individuals than institutions. Individual renewal is of great importance, and the quality of institutions is ultimately determined by the quality of their individual members. Individual renewal is also more familiar territory for educators and educational institutions, since the individual student has always been at least the target in the educational process, if not always an active participant. Educational institutions have less frequently shown concern for the other aspects of community renewal—for renewal of the institutions, organizations, and social, cultural, and political arrangements within the community. One reason is that educational institutions have not thought of themselves as agencies for social change, despite the many high-sounding phrases included in most statements of institutional purpose and philosophy. Most educational institutions and most educators have operated as though the teaching of particular subjects for which some marketable credentials can be awarded was the sole objective of the process of higher education. Education has usually been more a process of giving the learner a set of unquestioned facts, beliefs, or theories than one of helping the learner develop the ability to think, to reason, and to challenge such facts, beliefs, and theories. As Gardner (1964, p. 21) wrote, "All too often we have been giving our young people cut flowers when we should have been teaching them to grow their own plants."

Another reason we educators have been more concerned with individuals than with institutions is that we have not known how to go about the improvement of institutions and organizations that do not register at our colleges, attend our classes, graduate with degrees from our institutions, or fit into our statistics. The fact is that the educational improvement of community agencies and organizations can rarely be accomplished on our campuses at all. Unfortunately, the concept of the community-based college as an institution working cooperatively with and throughout the community and deriving from the needs of the community not only its purposes, programs, and direction but its very reason for being is, so far, more talked and written about than practiced.

The community renewal college must concern itself with the renewal of institutions as well as individuals in the community, for two important reasons. First, the community it serves is more than a collection of individuals operating independently of one another. The community consists of individuals who act in the context of cultural, social, and political institutions and organizations. To help the community renew and improve itself, we must assist with the renewal and improvement of all its working machinery—not only individuals alone but also individuals operating as groups. Second, the community renewal college is itself an institution in the community. As such, it must attend to its own continual renewal, or the inevitable process of aging will render it as ineffective as any institution. Fortunately, most of the strategies for renewal of other institutions in the community can also rejuvenate the college itself. Conversely, as the college becomes more adept at managing its own renewal, it will find that assisting other institutions in the community becomes easier.

Renewing People, Purposes, and Procedures

The many organizations in the typical community have varied functions and patterns of organization, but all have three aspects in common. First, the social institutions we are speaking of are composed of people. But rather than people acting only as individuals, they are people acting in the context of a purpose and an established way of working to achieve the purpose. Hence, an institution is more than the sum of its individual members. In addition to the members, there are external people who have a great effect upon the institution and who must be considered in the study of it. These people in the community who determine to a great extent the success or failure of the institution comprise its customers or consumers (both current and potential), its supporters, its possible detractors, and its potential members.

Second, each institution has a stated purpose or purposes. There may be purposes in addition to the officially adopted one. In fact, it may be that the unofficial purpose of the institution—the one reflected in its operation—is much more important than the stated purpose. It may be acceptable to have an unofficial working purpose that differs from the formally stated purpose, but it is a handicap if the purposes are not compatible or if members (and outsiders working with the institution) do not realize that there is a purpose other than the officially adopted one.

Third, each institution has a mode of operating, either officially established or developed and accepted through practice. The mode of operating may be formalized, as in an elaborate policy manual, or it may simply exist as an informal set of operating procedures. Again, it is important that those working in and with the institution understand how it goes about achieving its purposes.

Every institution or organization in the community, including the community college, can be described in terms of these three factors—its people, its purpose or purposes, and its established operating procedures. It is in terms of these three factors that the community renewal college must study itself and other organizations if it would help develop processes of continual institutional renewal.

To show promise as a target for renewal, an institution must be more than merely alive: it must also be reasonably healthy. Many institutions, including colleges, no longer vital in the sense of actively achieving a purpose, are kept alive artificially through loyalty of members, through tradition, through laws or other political devices, or simply because no one has pronounced them dead and made the final arrangements. Few institutions—again, including colleges— should expect eternal life; many, having achieved their purposes, should be terminated so that the people involved may get on to other business. Of course, institutions with important continuing purposes to achieve should not die untimely deaths or cease productive lives because of failure to renew themselves as vital, functioning institutions in a changing community.

An institution that would renew itself must constantly evaluate itself in terms of its most important resource—its people. The institution must ask the following questions about its internal and external people:

1. Who are the internal people of the institution? Are they suited to the *current* purposes of the institution? Are their numbers adequate and appropriate; if not, why not? Who are the potential members? What is the expressed power structure of the institution; if another power structure is the real one, what is it? What is the level of satisfaction of the members of the institution?

How flexible and creative are the people of the institution? Are they open to learning, adaptable to change in the institution, and responsive to the need for such change? Are they current in their thinking, their knowledge, and their skills and abilities? Are they attuned to the changing needs of the external people? What barriers to renewal do they have within themselves as individuals and what barriers have they erected collectively as members of the institution? Does the group welcome, tolerate, or reject dissenters within itself? Are the members—as individuals and as members of the institution—objective enough to see the need for change in themselves and in the institution?

2. What are the categories of external people upon whom the institution depends? Are these customers or consumers? Do other institutions protect the institution under study? Who supports the institution and how? Is this support appropriate and adequate? What is the level of satisfaction of the external people?

The institution must also constantly evaluate itself in terms of its purpose or purposes. The following questions are important:

1. What are the purposes of the institution? Are the real purposes the same as the stated ones? Are the real purposes understood and accepted by the internal and external people?

2. To what extent is the institution achieving its purposes? What would help the institution achieve its purposes more effectively?

3. Are the purposes of the institution relevant to the needs of the members and the community? Are there acceptable procedures for effecting change in the purposes of the institution as the community, the institution, or the members change? Are any of the purposes, either official or unofficial, themselves barriers to change and renewal? (For example, is one of the purposes to preserve the status quo of the institution? This may be an unofficial but real—and effectively achieved—purpose of a faculty senate.) Do the purposes themselves foster renewal of the organization? If not, can such a purpose be added to the existing ones?

Finally, the institution must evaluate itself with regard to the effectiveness of its established ways of working to achieve its purposes:

1. Are the ways in which the institution operates appropriate to the purposes of the institution? Are they appropriate to the needs of the internal and external people? Are they viewed as appropriate and effective by both groups? How could they be made more effective?

2. Are the internal and external communication processes of the institution effective? What are their strengths and limitations? How could they be made more effective?

3. Do the established operating procedures of the institution foster or inhibit institutional change and renewal? Do the members perceive that by working through the operating procedures they can effect change in the institution and in themselves? Do the operating procedures allow for maximum input from external people; if so, is this input used to improve the effectiveness of the institution? Do the operating procedures have built-in machinery for change of the procedures themselves as need arises either internally or externally?

Barriers to Self-Renewal

The community institution that would be self-renewing must constantly address itself to difficult and persistent problems. These problems will vary from institution to institution and from community to community. Unless they are solved at every level of the institution, adoption of new roles and dedication to new purposes will be mere facades covering outmoded edifices. The need to solve these problems should not be looked upon as a handicap or a detriment to institutional development. Continual soul-searching with regard to critical problems is a process necessary to renewal. As community-based colleges become more active in community renewal, we believe they will find it necessary to reexamine every aspect of their institutions and develop plans to produce needed change in them—from accreditation, affirmative action, articulation, and attrition to career education, collective bargaining, community-based programs, general education, governance, internal and external communications, learning assistance, organization and management, plant maintenance and utilization, and testing and counseling services. The following concerns, especially, may serve as barriers to institutional renewal.

External (Governmental) Governance Structures. During times of budgetary retrenchment, will legislators, who for the most part came up through traditional educational systems, retreat to a curriculum consisting of liberal arts plus some vocational education, eschewing newer community-oriented programs and services? Will local boards force commitments to full-time traditional faculty, to degree-credit programs, and to past practices to emerge at the top of the priority list when considering a standstill or shrinking budget?

Internal Governance Structures. With few exceptions, the teachers and administrators in internal governance structures (faculty senates, administrative committees, and so forth) are full-time staff members, representing traditional programs of study. Many of those involved in community renewal efforts are part-time or new, and have not broken into the traditional committees. The one segment of the internal college community that is perhaps best acquainted with community needs is frequently overlooked in the internal governance structure: the classified staff. How does a college that seeks to help renew the community turn around this tradition-dominated internal governance system? Can this be accomplished without implied threats that nudge the insecure toward unionization or other havens of the status quo? Is there room at every level of program and service activity for lay advisory committees or at least some kind of lay input beyond the present efforts in occupational training? And finally, how can a plan for governance and decision making be developed for a noncampus college, with its dispersed personnel and facilities? Many colleges that have attempted to establish nontraditional campuses, degree programs, or even courses report that the strongest opposition has come from the faculty (and sometimes administration) of the more-traditional arms of the colleges.

Senior-College and University Articulation. Senior colleges and universities have similar problems of internal governance, which are even more pronounced because the faculty in charge of curriculum and programs is more traditional and more entrenched. Will internal governance procedures make it difficult for universities to grant transfer credit for students' course work in community renewal? At the same time that community colleges are seeking to broaden their scope of responsibility and meet the challenge of community-renewal head on, senior colleges and universities are also questioning and testing their identity. Even major regional universities are looking more carefully at their local communities with a view to expanding their commitments to local services. How does the local community college, operating next door to such a senior institution, coordinate with that institution when trying to fulfill community needs?

Accreditation. How will the various accrediting bodies respond to community renewal activity? Will they adjust their standards for facilities, finances, and resources flexibly enough to accommodate the many facets of a community renewal program? Will the college that truly desires to achieve community renewal wait until its accrediting association changes and accommodates its activities, or will it push ahead, providing leadership for similar institutions that hold membership in the organization?

For colleges in multicollege districts and for universities awarding many nontraditional degrees, accreditation has been a serious problem. Nova University (in Florida), for example, requested permission to offer new external doctoral-degree programs. Its accrediting agency refused, allowing only that the proposed innovations be options within an existing program. Since nontraditional colleges in multicollege districts do not usually meet the accreditation standards established for traditional colleges, accreditation has been a serious barrier to community-based innovations in many districts.

The Image. The community-based college that assists in the self-renewal of individuals in the community will become a changed institution. Its prior image in the community and within the institution will need to be refashioned, or it may serve as a brake on further institutional change and development. Will the interpretation of the college's community renewal commitment within and without the institution be adequately attended to, and will the necessary public-relations efforts be focused on revising the image? Even more, will the results of early renewal activities be such that they will convert faculty and friends to the new concept?

Kellogg Community College (in Battle Creek, Michigan), for example, has developed a community-based college catalog as a means of communicating effectively to potential clients the practical aspects of what college can mean for them. Over 80,000 college catalogs were delivered to homes in the college service area in 1975–1976 through local newspapers.

Traditionalism. The community renewal college will face disapproval from some quarters on grounds of concern for academic respectability and credentialism. It will maintain the "highest" standards, because its standards will be based on what the community truly needs and what individuals aspire to accomplish. Competencies carefully developed by all involved will clearly show the accountability of both student and institution. Again, the public-relations program can be of value here. The college will have to help critics realize that training surgeons is of little value if we train no ambulance drivers.

Collective Bargaining. While collective-bargaining contracts purport to extend and expand benefits to employees, they normally restrict change in the educational process by forcing a preservation of the status quo or even a retrenchment to past traditionalism. Moreover, a bargaining unit drawn from the full-time faculty will most likely contain many liberal-arts, tradition-oriented instructors, whereas under internal governance structures many of the instructors in the newer, community-based programs are part-time. The hard question here is how the college will participate in the collective-bargaining process without allowing contractual agreements to handcuff the college's potential for expanding into a new area of possibilities for self-renewal of the individuals in the community.

Affirmative Action. Policies of affirmative action and equal opportunity have been an important force in pointing colleges toward a broader range of students. The colleges have discovered that many disadvantaged students need different approaches to learning. Will the college that seeks to provide community renewal be able to build upon its experiences in affirmative action and recognize that a number of people in the college's community require individualized attention? Will the college seek to expand its services to a broader range of clients who have traditionally been ignored by higher education—for example, the handicapped, the elderly, and ethnic minorities?

Faculty and Staff Development. The community renewal

college will find it necessary to prepare people to work in a free learning environment. Much development and retraining will be necessary so that the faculty and staff will approach the new learning environment with greater understanding and commitment. The great question during times of economic crunch and restrictive budgets is whether the college can and will recognize the need and commit the necessary resources to provide such development, since few states have established restricted funds for this purpose.

The challenge of staff development for institutions desiring to become community-based has been taken up by Nova University, which recognizes that resources beyond those available at the local level are frequently required. Nova is developing an external Ed.D. option with specialization in community-based education, with the help of a national panel of advisers, in connection with its field-based program for community college teachers and administrators. The requirements of the new option include six learning modules, six performance-based practicums, individualized evaluation reports, a major applied-research project, and three summer institutes, including an introductory three-day workshop. The three-year option incorporates several competency areas from the parent program: learning theory and curriculum development, applied educational research and evaluation, governance and educational policy systems, societal factors, management systems, and leadership and change.

General Education. Passing through a highly structured general-education program may produce an *educated* person, but not necessarily a *learning* person. Many programs of general education are actually somewhat archaic (the "unliberating liberal arts," as they have been called), and they consist mostly of a highly structured curriculum with little room for electives and great emphasis on memorization of facts that have little relevance to today's world. If we are going to deal with community clients as individuals, we should come to conceive of general education as the process in which the student works with the college to produce his or her own program based upon competencies already attained and those needed or desired. In fact, many practitioners in the community college field insist that the program of community services, properly constituted, represents the original nontraditional approach, and its diversified offerings, the true general education. Will the college meet this challenge by loosening general-education requirements so that students can have the greatest amount of flexibility in designing their own programs while attaining the basic academic competencies required for their educational goals?

Student Freedom of Choice. It will be difficult for educators to completely accept that freedom of choice by the learner means freedom not only in selecting course content but also in selecting the time and space in which to learn. This concept is related to the issue of general education, but focuses more on the scheduling of courses and the flexibility of delivery systems. Will the college's adherence to traditional scheduling patterns, based on the assumption that serious students will adjust their educational needs to available offerings, give way to scheduling that accommodates the student who, for example, works for a living or has family responsibilities? Such accommodations should include evening and weekend classes, for instance, or classes held in places of employment and centers of community activities such as libraries, community centers, and churches. Will the college provide flexible delivery systems? Will it capitalize on the technological and electronic developments that have provided audio and visual channels of communication so that it may step boldly forward and give a wider range of persons access to a relevant, competency-based curricular content that will truly help students to react and relate to the changing world?

Institutional Inertia. Large, complex organizations are difficult to move. The tendency of too many people is to seek the protection and comfort of the status quo. It is difficult to communicate to large numbers of people the objectives of organizational change and to convince them of the advantages of new policies, procedures, and work habits. Furthermore, any bold move brings about a chain reaction, causing change throughout an institution. An additional complication is that in a multiunit institution, feelings of independence and autonomy cause resistance to any coordinated overall direction. The important question here is, Will the community-based college and its staff be skillful enough to provide the leadership to mobilize the many parts of a college toward renewal? The task will require adept human relations, effective internal communications, and a carefully developed plan of action.

Peter Smith, president of the Community College of Vermont, faces an even greater communications problem in a college without the traditional institutional reference points of physical structure, where the campus is an abstraction and the students and faculty are unseen. He explains (1976, p. 70): "There's nothing to shake your fist at when you're angry, there's no place to retreat to when you're confused, and there is no physical image in your mind. It's easy to say that education is a process and a college is a series of processes designed to help students learn, but it's very difficult to maintain yourself personally and professionally in a world of processes."

Self-Examination for Self-Renewal

The areas listed above touch on a few of the difficult questions a college must answer as it examines its own potential for continual renewal. Each of these examples, as well as other existing and emerging issues, must be faced and analyzed with the following questions in mind: In what way does the issue facilitate or hinder continual renewal of the college? What can the college do to minimize the negative effects of the issue and maximize its positive effects? How can the college best effect self-renewal when faced with restrictive arrangements over which it has no control? Finally, what alternative systems and arrangements can the college create to foster institutional self-renewal?

Several colleges have realized the need for serious and probing self-study in order to maintain institutional renewal. Cuyahoga Community College in Cleveland, Ohio, the Metropolitan Community Colleges of Kansas City, Valencia Community College in Florida, and the San Mateo Community College District in California have recently undergone or are undergoing self-study by means of charrettes involving various levels of college employees, students, trustees, and community representatives. The purpose of most such workshops has been the development or redevelopment of mission statements, goals, and long-range plans for facilities and educational programs. The desired college/community relationship has been of utmost importance in determining the process and the results of each study. These colleges have all realized the necessity of continual self-renewal if they are to remain vital institutions in their communities. Wayne State University's Monteith College, in Detroit, and De Anza College's "minicollege," in California, represent efforts to create experimental change agents within existing colleges and universities. Other colleges, such as J. Sargeant Reynolds, in Richmond, Virginia, are deeply involved in renewal of community institutions.

CASE STUDY: J. SARGEANT REYNOLDS COMMUNITY COLLEGE

Enough state government employees live in metropolitan Richmond to populate the typical small city. Certainly these 35,000 people and their employer, the State of Virginia, form a substantial challenge for J. Sargeant Reynolds Community College (JSRCC), located in the capital.

Appropriate to its commitment as a community renewal college, JSRCC confronted this challenge in 1973, the second year of its existence. Its development of the "Orientation to State Government" course, and the ripple effect created thereby, fit the criteria of institutional renewal set forth in this chapter by (1) demonstrating the college's ability to adapt to new constituencies, since any session of the course may include a mix of entry-level employees and top management; (2) establishing working relationships with state government agencies at all levels; (3) developing a totally new program for state employees which is partially filling an ombudsman role for employees and serving as an interpretive mechanism for state personnel policies.

Operated under the aegis of the state Division of Personnel, with the sanction of the governor and cabinet, this is the only officially recognized general orientation course for new state employees.

The way the college developed this program is illustrative of how a community renewal college can translate input from the community into problems that can be solved. When the president, Wade Gilley, and the dean of community development, Martha Turnage, began brain-storming about establishing liaison with state government agencies, there was no specific plan. The basic idea was that since state government agencies made up a large segment of the community, some way should be found to establish a working relationship with them. During a conference, the training director of the state Division of Personnel, Albert F. Stem, shared with Gilley a comprehensive survey of personnel directors of all state agencies and commissions in which training needs had been identified. "These we can get a handle on fairly easily," Stem said. But with a look of bewilderment, he pointed to a two-foot stack of papers and pamphlets on his book-case. "See that!" he said. "For two years John Garber [director, Division of Personnel] has been telling me to develop an orientation course for agencies that aren't large enough to have their own train-ing divisions. I have nightmares about it."

A critical point in JSRCC's philosophy of community develop-ment is that the college's work with other community institutions should aim at helping them do something they need done but for some reason find difficult or impossible. It is essential in this ap-proach to take a global view and be more concerned with institu-tional development than with some particular interest of the col-lege's, realizing that ultimately they are inseparable.

Funding for the development of this project came from the intergovernmental Personnel Act, initiated to establish a cooperative movement of national and state governments to reform or strengthen personnel systems. In states, such as Virginia, where state agencies function with maximum autonomy, it is particularly important to have a forum for continual interpretation of personnel policies.

Betsy Curtler, who had a legal background and advanced training in English, was employed to write a personnel manual as the foundation of the course. She and Turnage worked closely on course development, including writing and producing a training film. Chancellor Dana B. Hamel of the Virginia Community College System saw the merit of the program and contributed the filming services courtesy of the state Department of Community Colleges.

The governor began the film with a speech succinctly out-lining the traditions and responsibilities incumbent upon employees of the Commonwealth of Virginia. Next, a panoramic view of the history and geography of the state painted broad brush strokes against which the members of a typical Virginia family encounter services of the state government in their daily lives. In all, services of fifty-two state agencies are covered in the film, some explicitly and some by implication. In order to emphasize this major effort to stimulate initiative, training, and dedication to public service, the developers of the "Orientation to State Government" course have entitled the film *You Are the Commonwealth,* and the student manual *You and the Commonwealth.*

Class participants gain accurate information on advantages of employment with the state and greater understanding of state policies for equal employment opportunity, affirmative action, grievance procedures, training opportunities, employee evaluation, performance pay increases, standard operating procedures, and opportunities available throughout state government. Throughout the course, subject areas include the executive-branch organizational structure and the function of agencies. Group exercises include team building, interagency cooperation, and working with supervisors.

A preview showing of the film was held for the press and agency heads. Then came several months of working with personnel directors of agencies during the pilot phase of the course to develop it in a way to meet a multiplicity of needs. These personnel directors suggested revisions and helped shape its final format. The succeeding months were spent in final rewriting of the personnel manual, establishing operating procedures for the two-day, ten-hour course, and opening lines of communication with as many of the state's 143 agencies and commissions as possible. By the end of the first full year of operation of the course, over 750 employees from sixty-six state agencies had taken the course—only 1 per cent of the potential market. No longer was it being aimed specifically at new employees; it had evolved into a course for employees at any level of job status and stage of experience. Germane to this evolutionary process is the cross-fertilization that results from the mix of employees in each session. Because of the exchange among participants, and the human-relations exercises employed, educational level and agency status become insignificant.

Now that the program has been recognized and established, it has become part of the Center for Management Development on JSRCC's downtown campus. Here it serves as a natural adjunct to other involvements of the college with state agencies. Among the ripple effects may be noted the following: (1) development of a course in administrative law for the Division of Motor Vehicles; (2) development of alternative methods of teaching courses for agencies large enough to assure full classes; (3) the practice by some personnel directors of considering course attendance in personnel evaluations; (4) use of *You Are the Commonwealth* as a recruitment tool for state employment and as a means of conveying information to the general public; (5) efforts by several other states to develop similar programs for their employees; (6) recognition of the college as a resource by state agencies; (7) a proposal by the state that the college conduct management training for women in secretarial and clerical positions in agencies; (8) a workshop held in cooperation with the Legislative Services Division, assisting the agency in drafting legislation; (9) exploratory conversations proposing "Commonwealth Community College" for state agencies, patterned after Air Force Community College.

"Orientation to State Government" has been a productive tool for institutional renewal. The Governor's Commission on Governmental Management maintains a close relationship with the course and follows with active interest the evaluations by participants.

Whereas universities are in a position to offer research assistance to state governmental agencies, community colleges are in a better position to help them increase the efficiency and effectiveness of their employees in pragmatic ways, as in "Orientation to State Government."

The two characteristics of colleges that appear to have the greatest effect on their capability for continual renewal are *flexibility* and *sensitivity*. Continual renewal mandates continual change or at least continual readiness for change. Whatever restricts the flexibility of the college or limits its ability to change as conditions change also prevents renewal of the college.

The Metropolitan Community Colleges of Kansas City, Missouri (see case study in Chapter Five), suggest the catalytic role that a new unit of a multicollege district may play for the entire system. The new fourth college, Pioneer Community College, provides opportunities for districtwide renewal in the areas of design and delivery of nontraditional instruction, staff development, and airway and video-package education. For example, faculty members from the three older colleges who are interested in furthering their professional development are assigned to Pioneer on a temporary basis to augment its small full-time staff.

The college that would help renew its community must be capable of adapting to new constitutencies as its programs reach different segments of the community, of developing new and different relationships with individuals and groups in the community, and of providing new programs and services as community needs change. In short, the college and the community should be engaged in a joint venture in which the college is capable of assuming any role or combination of roles deemed most feasible by both partners at any given time.

The joint-venture relationship also demands that the college be extremely sensitive to the changing problems and wishes of its community, so as to be able not only to respond immediately when called upon but also to anticipate needs and assume leadership in corrective action. Such a college must have a continuous flow of information from the community. Of even greater importance, however, it must also be able to translate great amounts of unorganized information into problems that can be solved, social or educational needs that can be met, competencies that can be developed, target groups that can be reached, and cultural and educational deficiencies that can be overcome. The college must know not only the needs of the community but also its strengths and its resources, and must be sensitive to the community's latent potential for self-improvement. The community renewal college is, in the simplest terms, a *student-oriented* institution that recognizes the total community as its student body and stands ready to meet the ever-changing needs of that student body.

VII

Colleges for the New America

◆◆◆◆◆◆◆◆◆◆◆◆◆◆◆◆◆◆◆◆◆◆◆◆◆◆◆◆◆◆◆◆◆◆◆◆◆

In the year after the victory at York-
town assured the independence of the thirteen colonies, Hector
St. John de Crèvecoeur, a Frenchman who became a naturalized
citizen of New York in 1765, published his *Letters from an American Farmer*. Letter number three describes his perception of the
process by which America would become a powerful nation: "He is
an American," St. John de Crèvecoeur wrote, "who, leaving behind
all his ancient prejudices and manners, receives new ones from the
new mode of life he has embraced, the new government he obeys,
and the new rank he holds. He becomes an American by being received in the broad lap of our great Alma Mater. Here individuals
of all nations are melted into a new race of men, whose labors and
posterity will one day cause great changes in the world. Americans
are the western pilgrims who are carrying along with them that

131

great mass of arts, sciences, vigor, and industry which began long since in the east; they will finish the great circle."

Not the least factor undergirding this early perception of Americans was an abiding faith in our traditions of courage, resourcefulness, persistence in the face of hardships, and achievement in spite of obstacles. The "western pilgrims" indeed carried into far places the culture and civilization of the Old World, but more than that, they created a civilization that is characteristic of themselves and no one else. The genius of this country during the two hundred years of its existence has been its independence and its capacity to assimilate other cultures and at the same time develop characteristics distinctly American.

Being distinctly American has sometimes drawn the scorn of sensitive souls who have accused Americans of gaucherie in far places. But at home, Americans have instituted movements that have grown to worldwide proportions. Among these was the movement for free public education first advanced by Thomas Jefferson, whose words are now engraved inside the Jefferson Memorial in Washington, D.C.: "Establish the law for educating the common people. This is the business of the state . . ." It remained for educators in the twentieth century to carry this distinctly American principle forward to include at least two years of higher education. Their efforts to educate more fully the "common people" marked the birth of the distinctly American educational institution, the community college.

Thomas Jefferson's fertile imagination not only shaped our form of government but laid the groundwork for a system of education unique in all the world. His home, Monticello, was so located on the crown of a little hill that he could stand at the north portico of the mansion and look across the countryside to the rotunda of his university. The university was his pride, and he considered its existence one of his greatest achievements. He was its founder, its architect, and its first president. In Jeffersonian democracy's terms, it was our first "people's college."

Today a new sight is to be seen from the north portico of Monticello, for on the smaller hill between Jefferson's home and his university stands Virginia Piedmont Community College. The symbolism of its location is graphic. If Jefferson were to stand on the north portico today and see this college arisen between him and the

University of Virginia, it would probably be more significant to him than it is to many of us. He would understand the natural changes that led from the European-style university of the eighteenth century through the land-grant institution of the nineteenth to the community college in the twentieth. He knew that an institution of education, in order to stay alive and productive, must be an organic part of society: when society changes, its public institutions must either change or be replaced. Today, both the University of Virginia and Piedmont Community College are viable, vibrant, responsive institutions, working with different clienteles and fulfilling different but equally important educative missions.

One hundred fifty years have passed since the University of Virginia opened, and for nearly a hundred of those years, higher education in America remained largely governed by a narrowly academic orientation that went better with an agrarian aristocracy than with the growing urban, industrial economic democracy. To help correct that deficiency, the community college was created. Recognizing that tyranny can survive only where ignorance prevails, democracy requires that each individual have the opportunity to be educated to the level of his highest potential. "If a nation expects to be ignorant and free," Jefferson reminded us in 1816, "it expects what never was and never will be." A participatory democracy requires an informed and educated citizenry, and therefore an educational system dedicated to the renewal of ordinary citizens and their communities.

Thirty years ago, Cousins called for society's reevaluation of itself in an atomic age. Observing that "man must consider himself in relation to his individual development," he stated (1974, pp. 59–60): "Once before, the world knew a Golden Age where the development of the individual—his mind and body—was considered the first law of life. In Greece, it took the form of the revolution of awareness, the emancipation of the intellect from the limitations of corroding ignorance and prejudice. Once again, if man wills it, he can be in a position to restore that first law of life. But he shall have to effect a radical transformation in his approach to and philosophy of education, which must prepare him for the opportunities and responsibilities not only of his chosen work but for the business of living . . . Education, like the mind itself, has no rigid boundaries."

Now the time has come for another "revolution of awareness"—awareness that education is continuous with life experience and not merely preparatory to it; awareness that it makes little difference where or how or at what age learning takes place, so long as it does take place and in circumstances appropriate to the learner; awareness that the "new students" are the primary responsibility of community-oriented colleges and that how successfully those colleges discharge that responsibility will be determined by the degree to which those students experience "the emancipation of the intellect from the limitations of corroding ignorance and prejudice."

The world, as we have known it, is coming to an end. Who could have believed that the doomsayers of the fifties and sixties were right about the rapid decline of natural resources and the explosion of population? How were we to prepare for the changes in our society within our life span? The answer is quite simple. We could not have prepared for the issues of change, but we could have been —and must learn to be—ready for change itself. One need only meet a disadvantaged minority person without the skills or abilities to participate in a society that has left him behind, or an elderly citizen subsisting on a pension check which diminishes daily in purchasing power and attempting to live in an environment he does not understand, to find people who have already lost most meaningful relationships with society and who perhaps are in danger of losing their identity as complete human beings. They and many others in our communities are in such precarious positions because they are no longer able to cope with a changing environment by changing—that is, renewing—themselves.

"Unless we attend to the requirements of renewal, aging institutions and organizations will bring our civilization to moldering ruin," Gardner wrote (1964, p. xvi). "Unless we cope with the ways in which modern society oppresses the individual, we shall lose the creative spark that renews both societies and men. Unless we foster versatile, innovative and self-renewing men and women, all the ingenious social arrangements in the world will not help us." Gardner believes that only individuals are capable of self-renewal and that only as our people are renewed can our social institutions be renewed. It is our belief that our communities and our higher-education institutions must become concerned with individual, institutional, and community renewal in order to survive.

Some community organizations are already active in renewal, and a few schools and colleges are assuming leadership roles in this effort. Mostly, however, it is individuals themselves who are recognizing the need for opportunities to renew themselves in order to cope with their daily existence and who are championing this revolution of awareness. What must happen is a coordination of efforts—a confluence of forces in which the self-interest of individuals, the needs of businesses and industries, the responsibilities of governmental agencies, and the purposes and resources of educational institutions come together to develop unified programs of community renewal. Such programs will have as their ultimate objective the improvement of community life through the renewed ability of individual citizens to participate in the affairs of the community, to cope successfully with continual social and cultural change, to contribute to the economic stability and well-being of the community as productive workers rather than liabilities, to partake of and contribute to our cultural heritage through worthwhile use of leisure time, and to collectively strengthen the various institutions and organizations that make up the community.

While many organizations in the community must participate to effect such renewal, the responsibility for assisting the movement and for coordinating the efforts of all is likely to fall to one. The American invention—the community college—reconceptualized as a community renewal college, is perhaps best prepared to assume this responsibility.

From a philosophical perspective, the community renewal college recognizes that education should be everywhere—rather than separate from the community. The only requirement of the setting is that the community be able to work and learn there. Community renewal education becomes a reality only when the community and the institution join together to decide upon such things as educational needs within the community. Such a philosophical perspective suggests that the college must be more than a formal institution with a defined campus and structured programs. The community and the college can no longer be side by side; they must instead be intermingled. The essence of serving individual and community needs can be found in the college's commitment to overcome the countless physical, psychological, and other barriers that keep students in the community from attending on-campus programs.

The community renewal college views itself as one agency among other social and civic agencies dedicated to human development and self-actualization. It assumes a special responsibility, however, in taking the initiative to touch the lives of all citizens, whether through direct or indirect services and activities, programs, and events. Community renewal education implies, more than anything else, a relationship between the college and the community in which the college derives its objectives and the resulting programs from the needs and wishes of the community, rather than one in which the college simply provides programs for the community. Motivating the community to use its facilities and resources as vehicles for educational improvement is an important challenge for the institution, its staff and faculty, and its programs. The community renewal college must become an educational arm of the community.

To do so, the community renewal college must be performance-oriented. That is, the competencies it develops must fit the needs of the learner rather than the expectations of the teacher, so that competencies are more important than grades or credits and so that the learner can measure his achievement of an objective in his own terms without reference to the teacher's evaluation of it. The welding student, for example, should learn to weld successfully; the English student should learn to construct a logical, mechanically correct paragraph. Such a college will place the individual above the institution: it will emphasize human needs rather than institutional needs.

This philosophical statement of the mission of the community renewal college cannot be implemented without a pragmatic set of principles and guidelines that can actualize this new approach to education. At least five steps are needed in this process:

1. *Identification of potential clientele to be served.* The college must determine the needs of the community—a procedure requiring active involvement of the institution with the community in order to find out what is going on and what the real needs are.

2. *Removal of barriers to access.* The college must ensure

that its facilities are available to those who compose the community. The facilities include the physical campus, if any, as well as the intangible campus represented by satellite centers and other environments for learning.

3. *Development of new avenues of access.* The college must cooperate with, and become a broker between, the community and the variety of agencies within the community that provide a potential for satisfying needs of individuals and groups. In other words, community renewal education requires the college to be an educational catalyst for the community and its citizens.

4. *Development of curriculums and services.* In addition to being a change agent in the community, the community renewal college must be adaptable and ready to change itself. Target groups can assist it in designing the strategies and delivery modes for instruction that will result in a comprehensive system of community education and service.

5. *Demonstration of its practicality and effectiveness.* The institution must be continually evaluating its own programs, its own responsibilities to the community, and its ability to serve the public. Using such evaluations, it must make decisions regarding its role as initiator, promoter, broker, or silent partner in the educational process.

In these ways, the community renewal college, dedicated to community service in all its programs, will offer a different kind of education for a different kind of student. It will offer a new model of education: one that is true to the integrity of the individual as well as the needs of society; one that is dedicated to human renewal, recognizing that only as individual obsolescence is prevented does the community tend to be renewed and restored. The mind does not grow old, it grows obsolete. That process begins the day we stop learning.

It has been said that there is no such thing as "higher" education: instead, education only gets broader and deeper. This idea epitomizes the need for institutions dedicated to *further* education rather than "higher" education: colleges that offer well-conceived, carefully developed learning experiences, both formal and informal, designed to facilitate and perpetuate individual self-renewal and social revitalization. Such institutions will enable us to achieve the mission of improving the quality of life in America's communities that Pifer (1974) has advocated for the community college, and to reverse the process of social decay feared by Gardner (1964) by developing an ever-renewing society within which continuous innovation, renewal, and rebirth can occur.

This mission of restoration and renewal will render obsolete such a modern "tale of two cities" as that of Kansas City, presented in a speech by C. D. Tucker (1974):

A Kansas City with its idyllic riverfront setting, its beautiful parks—and its ugly claustrophobic slums . . .

A Kansas City of fine mansions—and of miserable hovels . . .

A city of incredibly affluent suburbs . . . and condemned tenements . . .

A Kansas City of famous restaurants—and hungry people . . .

A city with the most attractive shopping center in the nation—and dilapidated mom-and-pop storefronts . . .

A city where several thousand young Future Farmers of America convened recently to map their careers while several thousand young blacks convened on the street corners to map their careers . . .

A Kansas City where so much is up to date, but a city which is also up to date in unemployment, in crime, in poor housing, in high school dropouts, in health care deficiencies . . .

In short, a city much like other urban centers—a city dedicated to citizenship—and to narrow self-interest, a city of rare promise—and faltering hope . . .

The community renewal college can lead the way in overcoming these inequities. It can provide models, develop exemplary programs, and demonstrate the effect of renewal to other institutions and agencies in its own community and in others throughout our nation.

The institution embarking upon such a role recognizes that renewal is a process, not a product. Its task can never be finished, for the concept of completion is the antithesis of renewal. Far from falling victim to disheartenment at the job never finished, the goal never achieved, the system never perfected, and the organization never worthy of permanence, such a college accepts the challenge of coping with the new, adapting to change, bringing an increasing number of citizens into participation in the stimulating events of their times, and helping its community revitalize itself. No educational institution has ever attempted a more stimulating and exciting task—or one more crucial to the very survival of its society.

Bibliographic Essay

The authors of this book have drawn primarily upon their collective breadth of experience and their harmony of philosophy. However, there exists a wealth of literature that is relevant to the various issues introduced in this book. An exhaustive bibliography would cover the entire field of higher education, as well as all other institutions, groups, and agencies that provide any kind of educational services. An attempt will be made here to mention only some of the major sources of reading that could prove useful to those interested in pursuing further the idea of community renewal. Publication data for the sources mentioned here can be found in the Bibliography.

The general idea of renewal is most thoughtfully and purposefully addressed by J. Gardner in *Self-Renewal: The Individual and the Innovative Society*. Gardner's influence is strongly felt by the authors of the present book. Also of value in planning renewing educational services is the book edited by futurist A. Toffler, *Learning for Tomorrow: The Role of the Future in Education.*

Several terms representing concepts related to community renewal and its allied activities have rapidly become household

141

words in postsecondary education. For example, the emerging concept "community-based education" is currently being addressed in community college periodicals, such as *Community and Junior College Journal, The Community College Review,* and *Community College Frontiers.* The term *community-based* was first introduced by E. J. Gleazer, Jr., in his article "After the Boom . . . What Now for the Community Colleges?" After the exploration of that question, Gleazer's follow-up challenge, "Beyond the Open Door: the Open College," firmly established the concept (as well as the name) of community-based education. *A Policy Primer for Community-Based Community Colleges: Report of the 1974 Assembly of the American Association of Community and Junior Colleges,* edited by C. R. Schenkman, summarizes policy discussions initiated by the association regarding new roles for community colleges.

Another emerging concept that has received wide attention is "lifelong learning." Two of the recent publications dealing with the concept are *Patterns for Lifelong Learning: A Report of Explorations Supported by the W. K. Kellogg Foundation,* by T. M. Hesburgh and others, and *Lifelong Learners—A New Clientele for Higher Education,* edited by D. W. Vermilye. Both books provide reports of lifelong learning programs that the reader may place in the history of community renewal.

The term *nontraditional* has been around somewhat longer than *community-based* and *lifelong learning,* but the varied ideas presented in articles and books on nontraditional education are well worth pursuing for readers interested in developing institutions for community renewal. One such volume on this topic is *Planning Non-Traditional Programs: An Analysis of the Issues for Postsecondary Education,* by K. P. Cross and others. Not only does the book give a good overview of the varied dimensions of nontraditional programs in postsecondary education, it contains an exceptional annotated bibliography, which gives the reader a rich guide to further study.

Concepts that are related to "nontraditional," such as "open university," "university without walls," and "external degree," may be pursued in *The External Degree,* by C. O. Houle. Although published as a separate book, it is a part of the report of the Commission on Non-Traditional Study that resulted in the publication of

Diversity by Design. Houle's work includes an excellent bibliographic essay on the many sources related to this broad area.

Programs of community services have been implemented in educational institutions across the land. A wealth of literature in the form of journal articles is available on this function of education; the reader's attention should be directed to some of the few books that cover this field. E. L. Harlacher's *Community Dimension of the Community College* thoroughly describes community services, giving examples and predicting trends. A section of *Perspectives on the Community-Junior College* (W. K. Ogilvie and M. R. Raines, Eds.) devotes several pages to the topic, and G. A. Myran's *Community Services in the Community College* is another good source of current information on community services.

An adequate amount of literature on the topic of community-needs assessment does not exist. H. B. C. Spiegel briefly addresses the topic in his article "Assessing Community Needs: An Analytical Framework," in the previously mentioned *Policy Primer for Community-Based Community Colleges* (C. R. Schenkman, Ed.). Spiegel recommends as "an old standby" R. L. Warren's *Studying Your Community*. Some systematic approaches to needs assessment—though generally limited to vocational or career education—which are excellent examples of new efforts in the area are reported by K. D. Tucker, of the Central Florida Community Colleges Consortium, Orlando.

A number of publications are now emerging that deal with the characteristics and needs of students. In *Beyond the Open Door: New Students to Higher Education*, K. P. Cross analyzes the problems and characteristics of the "new students" who enter the "open door" to higher education. She gives particular attention to the special problems of ethnic minorities and women. A further example of the analysis of student target groups now being developed is a report of the Carnegie Commission on Higher Education, *Opportunities for Women in Higher Education*. This volume deals not only with women students but with women employed in higher education.

On the topic of cooperating with various groups, one book should receive special attention: *Community Education: A Developing Concept*, by M. F. Seay and associates. Not only does the volume trace the development of the "community schools" concept into the "community education" concept, it ideals in depth with the various institutions, committees, and agencies involved in community education. The *Community Education Journal* provides an up-to-date account of the community education and community school movements with articles of pragmatic interest to the practitioner. Special attention should be given to the January-February 1975 issue, which contains a number of articles on the topic of community education and community/college cooperation. For the topic of promoting the community college's leadership role in coordinating the efforts of community agencies, the reader is directed to A. Pifer's speech "Community College and Community Leadership."

While "competency-based" education has been around for some time now, often called by such terms as *performance-based* and *mastery learning,* most of the literature deals with the process rather than the content of competency achievement. As an approach to this body of literature, the authors suggest that the reader begin with *A Modest Proposal: Students Can Learn,* by J. E. Roueche and J. C. Pitman; B. Bloom's "Mastery Learning and Its Implications for Curriculum Development," in *Confronting Curriculum Reform,* edited by E. W. Eisner; and *Accent on Learning: Improving Instruction and Reshaping Curriculum,* by K. P. Cross. References cited in these sources will lead to additional exploration.

The many issues that present potential barriers to community renewal are being raised and analyzed in the literature, especially in the journals. Several such issues are identified in *College Responses to Community Demands: The Community College in Challenging Times,* by A. M. Cohen and associates. *New Colleges for New Students,* by L. Hall and associates, describes many institutions that are eagerly and successfully tearing down barriers and discovering new dimensions of access by the "new students."

Bibliography

The Black Community and the Community College: Action Programs for Expanding Opportunity, a Project Report. Atlanta, Ga.: Southern Regional Education Board, Institute for Higher Educational Opportunity, 1970.

BLOCKER, C. E., and BACON, J. N. "The Community College of the Future: A Balancing Act Between Social and Educational Demands." *Community College Review,* 1973, *1*(3), 7–13.

BLOOM, B. "Mastery Learning and Its Implications for Curriculum Development." In E. W. Eisner (Ed.), *Confronting Curriculum Reform.* Boston: Little, Brown, 1971.

BOGUE, J. *The Community College.* New York: McGraw-Hill, 1950.

BOONE, E. J. "Adult Education: A Quest for Life." *Community College Review,* 1973, *1*(1), 6–13.

BOYER, E. L. "Breaking Up the Youth Ghetto." In D. W. Vermilye (Ed.), *Lifelong Learners—A New Clientele for Higher Education.* San Francisco: Jossey-Bass, 1974.

BOYER, M. A. "An ERIC Review: Meeting the Problems of Student Recruitment." *Community College Review,* 1975a, *3*(2), 78–81.

BOYER, M. A. "An ERIC Review: Unique Approaches to Community Services." *Community College Review,* 1975b, *2*(4), 74–77.

BOYER, M. A. "Non-Traditional Education in Two-Year Colleges." *Community College Frontiers,* 1975c, *4*(1), 46–51.

BROWN, G. I. *Human Teaching for Human Learning: An Introduction to Confluent Education*. New York: Viking, 1971.

BROWNELL, B. *The College and the Community*. New York: Harper & Row, 1952.

BRUNER, J. S. *The Process of Education*. Cambridge, Mass.: Harvard University Press, 1960.

BUSHNELL, D. S. *Organizing for Change: New Priorities for Community Colleges*. New York: McGraw-Hill, 1973.

CAMPBELL, R. F., and RAMSEYER, J. A. *The Dynamics of School Community Relationships*. Boston: Allyn and Bacon, 1955.

CARNEGIE COMMISSION ON HIGHER EDUCATION. *The Campus and the City: Maximizing Assets and Reducing Liabilities*. New York: McGraw-Hill, 1972.

CARNEGIE COMMISSION ON HIGHER EDUCATION. *Opportunities for Women in Higher Education*. New York: McGraw-Hill, 1973a.

CARNEGIE COMMISSION ON HIGHER EDUCATION. *Toward a Learning Society: Alternative Channels to Life, Work and Service*. New York: McGraw-Hill, 1973b.

CLARK, B. R. *Adult Education in Transition: A Study of Institutional Insecurity*. Berkeley: University of California Press, 1958.

COHEN, A. M. *Dateline '79: Heretical Concepts for the Community College*. Beverly Hills, Calif.: Glencoe Press, 1969.

COHEN, A. M. "The Community College at the Millenium." *Community College Frontiers*, 1976, *4*(3), 42–46.

COHEN, A. M., and associates. *A Constant Variable: New Perspectives on the Community College*. San Francisco: Jossey-Bass, 1971.

COHEN, A. M., and associates. *College Responses to Community Demands: The Community College in Challenging Times*. San Francisco: Jossey-Bass, 1975.

COHEN, A. M., and BRAWER, F. B. "The Community College in Search of Identity." *Change*, Winter 1971–1972, *3*, 55–59.

COLEMAN, R. P., and NEUGARTEN, B. L. *Social Status in the City*. San Francisco: Jossey-Bass, 1971.

COMMISSION ON NON-TRADITIONAL STUDY. *Diversity by Design*. San Francisco: Jossey-Bass, 1973.

COMMISSION ON NON-TRADITIONAL STUDY. "Recommendations." *The Chronicle of Higher Education*, 1973, *8*(18), 6.

Community Education Journal. Midland, Mich.: Pendell, Jan.–Feb. 1975.

Continuing Education of Women. Washington, D.C.: Adult Education Association of the USA, 1970.

COUSINS, N. "Modern Man Is Obsolete." In R. L. Tobin (Ed.), *The Golden Age: The Saturday Review 50th Anniversary Reader.* New York: Bantam, 1974.

CROSS, K. P. *Occupationally Oriented Students.* Washington, D.C.: American Association of Junior Colleges, 1970.

CROSS, K. P. *Beyond the Open Door: New Students to Higher Education.* San Francisco: Jossey-Bass, 1971.

CROSS, K. P. *Accent on Learning: Improving Instruction and Reshaping the Curriculum.* San Francisco: Jossey-Bass, 1976.

CROSS, K. P., VALLEY, J. R., and associates. *Planning Non-Traditional Programs: An Analysis of the Issues for Postsecondary Education.* San Francisco: Jossey-Bass, 1969.

DALKEY, N. C. *The Delphi Method: An Experimental Study of Group Opinion.* Santa Monica, Calif.: The RAND Corporation, 1974.

DARKENWALD, G. G., and MEZIROW, J. *Post-Secondary Continuing Education: An Annotated Selected Bibliography.* New York: Center for Adult Education, Teachers College, Columbia University, 1974.

DEWEY, J. *Democracy and Education: An Introduction to the Philosophy of Education.* New York: Free Press, 1916.

DRUCKER, P. F. *The Age of Discontinuity: Guidelines to Our Changing Society.* New York: Harper & Row, 1969.

DUNN, R., and DUNN, K. *Practical Approaches to Individualizing Instruction: Contracts and Other Effective Teaching Strategies.* West Nyack, N.Y.: Parker Publishing Co., 1972.

DURANT, W. *The Story of Philosophy.* New York: Simon & Schuster, 1926.

ECKLEIN, J., and LAUFFER, A. *Community Organizers and Social Planners.* New York: Wiley, 1972.

ENSIGN, M. D. "Business-College Partnerships with Results." *Community and Junior College Journal,* 1975, *45*(4), 20–21.

FARMER, J. A., JR., and others. *Developing Community Service and Continuing Education Programs in California Higher Education Institutions.* Sacramento: California Coordinating Council for Higher Education, 1972.

FIEDLER, F. *A Theory of Leadership Effectiveness.* New York: McGraw-Hill, 1967.

FIELDS, R. R. *The Community College Movement.* New York: McGraw-Hill, 1952.

FISCHER, O. R., JR., and GOLLATTSCHECK, J. F. "Valencia Community College as an Educational Cooperative." *Community and Junior College Journal,* 1974, *45*(2), 12–15.

FISCHER, O. R., JR., and GOLLATTSCHECK, J. F. "Community Education: The College and Local Agencies." *The Community Services Catalyst,* Spring 1976, 67–69.

FLORIDA JUNIOR COLLEGE INTER-INSTITUTIONAL RE-SEARCH COUNCIL. *Post-Secondary Occupational Education in Florida—Planning, Implementation, Evaluation.* Gainesville, 1972.

FURNISS, W. T. *External Degrees: An Initial Report.* Washington, D.C.: American Council on Education, 1971a.

FURNISS, W. T. *Higher Education for Everybody?* Washington, D.C.: American Council on Education, 1971b.

GARDNER, J. W. *Excellence: Can We Be Equal and Excellent Too?* New York: Harper & Row, 1961.

GARDNER, J. W. *Self-Renewal: The Individual and the Innovative Society.* New York: Harper & Row, 1964.

GASS, J. R. "Lifelong Learning in Europe." In D. W. Vermilye (Ed.), *Lifelong Learners—A New Clientele for Higher Education.* San Francisco: Jossey-Bass, 1974.

GLEAZER, E. J., JR. "AACJC Approach: Summer Community Services." *Junior College Journal,* 1968a, *38,* 9.

GLEAZER, E. J., JR. *This Is the Community College.* Boston: Houghton Mifflin, 1968b.

GLEAZER, E. J., JR. "After the Boom . . . What Now for the Community Colleges?" *Community and Junior College Journal,* 1974a, *44*(4), 6–11.

GLEAZER, E. J., JR. "Beyond the Open Door: The Open College." *Community and Junior College Journal,* 1974b, *45*(1), 6–12.

GLEAZER, E. J., JR. *Project Focus: A Forecast Study of Community Colleges.* New York: McGraw-Hill, 1975.

GLEAZER, E. J., JR. (Ed.) *An Introduction to Junior Colleges.* Washington, D.C.: American Association of Junior Colleges, 1960.

Goals and Priorities for Jacksonville. A report compiled by the Commission on Goals and Priorities of the Community Planning Council, 1974.

GOLLATTSCHECK, J. F., and EVANS, D. L. "Reaching Communities via Television and Radio: The Florida Model." *Community and Junior College Journal,* 1976, *46*(6), 6–8.

GOLLATTSCHECK, J. F., and FISCHER, O. R., JR. "The Community College as an Education Cooperative." *The Community Services Catalyst,* Fall 1974, 1–6.

GOLLATTSCHECK, J. F., and FISCHER, O. R., JR. "Open Campus: For Anyone, Anytime, Anyplace." *Florida Schools,* April 1975, 8–11.

GOODLAD, J. I., and others. *The Changing School Curriculum.* New York: Fund for the Advancement of Education, 1966.

GOULD, S. B., and CROSS, K. P. (Eds.) *Explorations in Non-Traditional Study.* San Francisco: Jossey-Bass, 1972.

GRINNELL, J. E., and YOUNG, R. J. *The School and the Community.* New York: Ronald Press, 1955.

HALL, L., and associates. *New Colleges for New Students.* San Francisco: Jossey-Bass, 1974.

HAMLIN, H. M. *Citizens' Committees in the Public Schools.* Danville, Ill.: Interstate, 1952.

HARLACHER, E. L. "California's Community Renaissance." *Junior College Journal,* 1964a, *34,* 14–18.

HARLACHER, E. L. *Measuring the Public Image (Opinions and Attitudes) of the Community College.* Norwalk, Calif.: Cerritos College, 1964b.

HARLACHER, E. L. *A Program of Community Services for Cerritos College.* Community Services Study Report No. V. Norwalk, Calif.: Cerritos College, 1964c.

HARLACHER, E. L. *Effective Junior College Programs of Community Services: Rationale, Guidelines, Practices.* Occasional Report No. 10, Junior College Leadership Program. Los Angeles: University of California, 1967.

HARLACHER, E. L. "Community College Programs." In A. S. Knowles (Ed.), *Handbook of College & University Administration.* New York: McGraw-Hill, 1968a.

HARLACHER, E. L. "New Directions in Community Services: What's Past Is Prologue." *Junior College Journal,* 1968b, *38*(6), 12–17.

HARLACHER, E. L. *The Community Dimension of the Community College.* Englewood Cliffs, N.J.: Prentice-Hall, 1969.

HARLACHER, E. L. "Community Service in the Community: A New Dimension in Adult Education." In M. S. Knowles (Ed.), *Handbook of Adult Education in the USA.* Washington, D.C.: Adult Education Association of the U.S.A., 1970.

HARLACHER, E. L. "Community Services in the Community College." In L. C. Deighton (Ed.), *Encyclopedia of Education.* New York: MacMillan and Free Press, 1971.

HARLACHER, E. L. "Community Renewal College." *The Community Services Catalyst,* Fall 1973, 5–9.

HARLACHER, E. L. "Community Renewal College." In *National Conference on Community Continuing Education: Alternative Approaches to Responsibility.* Occasional Report No. 19, UCLA Community College Leadership Program. Los Angeles: University of California, 1974.

HARLACHER, E. L. "Brookdale Community College." *Management by Objectives in Higher Education: Theory, Cases & Implementation.* Durham, N.C.: National Laboratories for Higher Education, 1975.

HARLACHER, E. L., and ROBERTS, E. "Accountability for Student Learning." *Junior College Journal,* March 1971, 27–30. Reprinted in R. W. Hostrop (Ed.), *Accountability for Educational Results.* Hamden, Conn.: Linnet Books, 1973a.

HARLACHER, E. L., and ROBERTS, E. "Differentiated Staffing, Patterns and Potentials." In R. Yarrington (Ed.), *New Staff and New Student.* Washington, D.C.: American Association of Community and Junior Colleges, National Assembly, 1973b.

HEATHERS, G. *The Strategy of Educational Reform.* New York: New York University, School of Education, 1961.

HENRY, N. B. (Ed.) *The Public Junior College.* Fifty-fifth Yearbook of the National Society for the Study of Education. Chicago: University of Chicago Press, 1956.

HENRY, N. B. (Ed.) *Individualizing Instruction.* Sixty-first Yearbook of the National Society for the Study of Education, Part I. Chicago: University of Chicago Press, 1962.

HESBURGH, T. M., MILLER, P. A., and WHARTON, C. R., JR. *Patterns for Lifelong Learning: A Report of Explorations Supported by the W. K. Kellogg Foundation.* San Francisco: Jossey-Bass, 1973.

HILLWAY, T. *The American Two-Year College.* New York: Harper & Row, 1958.

HOENNINGER, R., and BLACK, R. A. "The Need for the Community College Without Walls." *Community College Review,* 1974, 2(2), 58–64.

HOLCOMB, H. M. (Ed.) *New Directions for Community Colleges.* San Francisco: Jossey-Bass, 1976.

HOLLEB, D. B. *Social and Economic Information for Urban Planning.* Chicago: Center for Urban Studies, University of Chicago, 1970.

HOLY, T. C., and SEMANS, H. H. *A Restudy of the Needs of California in Higher Education.* Sacramento: California State Department of Education, 1956.

HOULE, C. O. "Community Education Service: An Emerging Function of Higher Education." *Proceedings of the Institute for Administrative Offices of Higher Institutions,* 1948, 5–13.

HOULE, C. O. *Major Trends in Higher Adult Education.* Chicago: CSLEA, 1959.

HOULE, C. O. "The Obligation of the Junior College for Community Service." *Junior College Journal,* 1960, *30,* 502–516.

HOULE, C. O. *The External Degree.* San Francisco: Jossey-Bass, 1973.

HUCKFELDT, V. E. *A Forecast of Changes in Post-Secondary Education.* Boulder, Colo.: Western Interstate Commission for Higher Education, 1972.

HUNTER, B., and others. *Learning Alternatives in U.S. Education: Where Students and Computer Meet.* Englewood Cliffs, N.J.: Educational Technology Publications, 1974.

HUTCHINS, R. M. *The Learning Society.* New York: New American Library, Mentor, 1968.

JOHNSTONE, J. W. C., and RIVERA, R. J. *Volunteers for Learning.* Chicago: Aldine, 1965.

JOINT COMMITTEE ON THE CALIFORNIA MASTER PLAN FOR HIGHER EDUCATION. "California's New Segment?" *The Community Services Catalyst,* Spring 1974.

KAPLAN, A. "Fifth Dimension in American Education: Adult Education." *Educational Forum,* 1962, *36,* 133–142.

KAPRAUN, E. D. *Community Services in the Community College: A Bibliography.* Charlottesville: University of Virginia Center for Higher Education, 1973.

KATZ, D., and KAHN, R. L. *The Social Psychology of Organizations.* New York: Wiley, 1966.

KIPLINGER, A. *The Kiplinger Washington Letter,* 1976, *53*(3).

KNOELL, D., and MC INTYRE, C. *Planning Colleges for the Community.* San Francisco: Jossey-Bass, 1974.

KNOWLES, M. S. *The Adult Education Movement in the United States.* New York: Holt, Rinehart and Winston, 1962.

KNOWLES, M. S. *Higher Adult Education in the United States: The Current Picture, Trends and Issues.* Washington, D.C.: American Council on Education, 1969.

KNOWLES, M. S. *The Modern Practice of Adult Education: Androgogy vs. Pedagogy.* New York: Association Press, 1970.

KORIM, A. S. *Older Americans and Community Colleges: A Guide for Program Implementation.* Washington, D.C.: U.S. Dept. of HEW, Administration on Aging, 1974a.

KORIM, A. S. *Older Americans and Community Colleges: An Overview.* Washington, D.C.: U.S. Dept. of HEW, Administration on Aging, 1974b.

KREPS, J. M., and LAWS, R. *Training and Retraining Older Workers: An Annotated Bibliography.* New York: National Council on the Aging, 1976.

LACKEY, K. *Community Development Through University Extension.* Community Development Publication No. 3. Carbondale: Southern Illinois University, 1960.

LAMAR, A. L., JR. "A Black Educator's Perspective: How the Black Student Perceives the Community College." *Community College Review,* 1974, *1*(4), 41–46.

LANGSDORF, W. B. *Manual of Policies and Procedures for Preparation of Proposals and Administration of Pilot External Degree Programs.* Los Angeles: The California State University and Colleges, 1973.

LETARTE, C. E., and MINZEY, J. D. *Community Education: From Program to Process.* Midland, Mich.: Pendell, 1972.

LIVERIGHT, A. A., and MOSCONI, D. L. *Continuing Education in the United States: A New Survey.* New York: Association for Educational Development, 1971.

LYMAN, R. W. "The Search for Alternatives." *Educational Record,* Fall 1974, 218–219.

MARLAND, S. P., JR. *Career Education: A Proposal for Reform.* New York: McGraw-Hill, 1974.

MAYESKE, B. J. "Open University in America." In D. W. Vermilye (Ed.), *Lifelong Learners—A New Clientele for Higher Education.* San Francisco: Jossey-Bass, 1974.

MEAD, M. "A Redefinition of Education." *National Education Association Journal,* 1959, *48*, 15–17.

MEAD, M. *Culture and Commitment.* New York: Doubleday, 1971.

MEDSKER, L. *The Junior College: Progress and Prospect.* New York: McGraw-Hill, 1960.

MEYER, P. *Awarding College Credit for Non-College Learning: A Guide to Current Practices.* San Francisco: Jossey-Bass, 1975.

MILKOVICH, G. T., ANNON, A. J., and MAHONES, T. A. "The Use of Delphi Procedure in Manpower Forecasting." *Management Science,* 1972, *18*.

MILLER, P. A. "In Anticipation of the Learning Community." *Adult Leadership,* 1969, *17,* 306–308.

MINIKAN, N. "Commitment to a Community." *Perspectives in Education,* 1970, *3,* 16–26.

MOORE, W., JR. *Against the Odds: The High-Risk Student in the Community College.* San Francisco: Jossey-Bass, 1970.

MORTON, J. R. *University Extension in the United States.* University: University of Alabama Press, 1953.

MYRAN, G. A. "Community Services: An Emerging Challenge for the Community College." Working Paper No. 1. Washington, D.C.: American Association of Junior Colleges, 1969a.

MYRAN, G. A. *Community Services in the Community College.* Washington, D.C.: American Association of Community and Junior Colleges, 1969b.

MYRAN, G. A. "Community Services: Issues, Challenges and Perspective." In *Beyond the Open Door, The Open College: A Report on the National Conference on Community Services and the Community College.* Orlando, Fla.: Valencia Community College, 1974.

NIBLETT, W. R. (Ed.) *Higher Education: Demand and Response.* San Francisco: Jossey-Bass, 1970.

The 1970 Census and You. (Rev. ed.) Washington, D.C.: U.S. Dept., of Commerce, 1973.

O'BANION, T., and THURSTON, A. (Eds.) *Student Development Programs in the Community Junior College.* Englewood Cliffs, N.J.: Prentice-Hall, 1972.

OGILVIE, W. K., and RAINES, M. R. (Eds.) *Perspectives on the Community-Junior College.* New York: Meredith, 1971.

PALOLA, E. G., and OSWALD, A. R. *Urban Multi-Unit Community Colleges: Adaptation for the '70's.* Berkeley: Center for Research and Development in Higher Education, University of California, 1972.

PARKE, H. H., and HALL, J. F. "Functional Community Philosophy of Education." *Educational Digest,* 1971, *36,* 26–28.

PATTERSON, F. *Colleges in Consort: Institutional Cooperation Through Consortia.* San Francisco: Jossey-Bass, 1974.

PAULSTON, R. G. *Non-Formal Education.* New York: Praeger, 1972.

PEDDIWELL, J. A. *The Saber-Tooth Curriculum.* New York: McGraw-Hill, 1939.

PERLMAN, R., and GURIN, A. *Community Organization and Social Planning.* New York: Wiley, 1972.

PETERSEN, R., and PETERSEN, W. *University Adult Education: A Guide to Policy.* New York: Harper & Row, 1960.

PIERCE, T., MERRILL, E. G., WILSON, C., and KIMBROUGH, R. B. *Community Leadership for Public Education.* Englewood Cliffs, N.J.: Prentice-Hall, 1955.

PIFER, A. "Community College and Community Leadership." *Community and Junior College Journal,* 1974, *44*(8), 23–26.

PUNKE, H. H. *Community Use of School Facilities.* New York: King's Crown Press, 1951.

RAINES, M. R. *Life-Centered Education.* Research and Report Series, Report No. 6, Kellogg Community Services Leadership Program. East Lansing: Michigan State University, 1974.

REICH, C. A. *The Greening of America.* New York: Random House, 1970.

REYNOLDS, J. W. *An Analysis of Community Service Programs of Junior Colleges.* Washington, D.C.: U.S. Office of Education, 1960.

REYNOLDS, J. W. "Community Services." In N. B. Henry (Ed.), *The Public Junior College.* Chicago: University of Chicago Press, 1956.

REYNOLDS, J. W. "Community Colleges and Studies of Communities." *Junior College Journal,* 1970, *31,* 63–64.

RITTENBUSH, P. C. (Ed.) *Let the Entire Community Become Our University.* New York: Prometheus/Acropolis Press.

ROSS, B. H. *University-City Relations: From Coexistence to Cooperation.* Washington, D.C.: ERIC/AAHE Research Report No. 3, 1973.

ROUECHE, J. E. "Can Mastery Learning Be Humane? The Case for Performance-Based Instruction." *Community College Review,* 1975, *3*(1), 14–21.

ROUECHE, J. E., HERRSCHER, B. R., and BAKER, G. A., III. *Time As the Variable, Achievement As the Constant: Competency-Based Instruction in the Community College.* "Horizons Issues" Monograph Series; American Association of Community and Junior Colleges/Council of Universities and Colleges/ERIC Clearinghouse for Junior Colleges, 1976, 5.

ROUECHE, J. E., and KIRK, R. W. *Catching Up: Remedial Education.* San Francisco: Jossey-Bass, 1973.

ROUECHE, J. E., and LAFORGE, R. "Causing Learning in the Community College: The Recipe." *Community College Review,* 1974, *2*(1), 42–52.

ROUECHE, J. E., and PITMAN, J. C. *A Modest Proposal: Students Can Learn.* San Francisco: Jossey-Bass, 1972.

ST. JOHN DE CRÈVECOEUR, H. *Letters From an American Farmer,* 1782. Reprinted in L. B. Wright and H. T. Swedenberg (Eds.), *The American Tradition.* New York: Appleton-Century-Crofts, 1940.

SARASON, S. B. *The Creation of Settings and the Future Societies.* San Francisco: Jossey-Bass, 1972.

SCHENKMAN, C. R. (Ed.) *A Policy Primer for Community-Based Community Colleges: Report of the 1974 Assembly of the American Association of Community and Junior Colleges.* Washington, D.C.: American Association of Community and Junior Colleges, 1975.

SEAY, M. F., and associates. *Community Education: A Developing Concept.* Midland, Mich.: Pendell, 1974.

SEAY, M. F., and CRAWFORD, F. N. *The Community School and Community Self-Improvement.* Lansing, Mich.: Clair L. Taylor, Superintendent of Public Instruction, 1954.

SHARON, A. T. *College Credit for Off-Campus Study.* Washington, D.C.: ERIC/AAHE, 1971.

SHEATS, P., JAYNE, C. D., and SPENCE, R. B. (Eds.) *Adult Education: The Community Viewpoint.* New York: Dryden Press, 1953.

SILBERMAN, C. E. *Crisis in the Classroom.* New York: Random House, Vintage, 1970.

SMITH, G. K. (Ed.) *New Teaching, New Learning: Current Issues in Higher Education.* San Francisco: Jossey-Bass, 1971.

SMITH, P. P. "College Without a Campus." In A. M. Cohen and F. B. Brawer (Eds.), *New Directions for Community Colleges: Changing Managerial Perspectives,* no. 13. San Francisco: Jossey-Bass, 1976.

SMITH, R. M., AKER, G. F., and KIDD, R., JR. (Eds.) *Handbook of Adult Education.* Washington, D.C.: Adult Education Association of the USA, 1972.

SPIEGEL, H. B. C. "Assessing Community Needs: An Analytical Framework." In C. R. Schenkman (Ed.), *A Policy Primer for Community-Based Community Colleges: Report of the 1974 Assembly of the American Association of Community and Junior Colleges.* Washington, D.C.: American Association of Community and Junior Colleges, 1975.

STROTHER, G. B. "Open Education: Breaking the Barriers." *NUEA Spectator,* Sept. 1972, 10–13.

SWANSON, B. E., and LINDLEY, C. "College and Community: The Reciprocity of Change." *Adult Leadership*, 1970, *19*, 45–46.

THORNTON, J. W., JR. *The Community Junior College.* New York: Wiley, 1960.

THORNTON, J. W., JR., and BROWN, J. W. (Eds.) *New Media & College Teaching.* Washington, D.C.: National Education Association, 1968.

TOFFLER, A. *Future Shock.* New York: Bantam, 1970.

TOFFLER, A. (Ed.) *Learning for Tomorrow: The Role of the Future in Education.* New York: Random House, 1974.

TOLLEFSON, A. L. *New Approaches to College Student Development.* New York: Behavioral Publications, 1975.

TOTTEN, W. F. "Community Education: Best Hope for Society." *School and Society,* 1970a, *98,* 410–13.

TOTTEN, W. F. *Power of Community Education.* Midland, Mich.: Pendell, 1970b.

Toward the Open University: External Degree Opportunities. Buffalo, N.Y.: State University of New York at Buffalo, Division of Continuing Education, 1971.

TRIVETT, D. A. *Academic Credit for Prior Off-Campus Learning.* ERIC/AAHE Research Report No. 2, 1975.

TROUTT, R. *Special Degree Programs for Adults: Exploring Non-Traditional Degree Programs.* ACT Special Report No. 4, 1971.

TUCKER, C. D. (Secretary of State, State of Pennsylvania) Speech before the Kansas City, Missouri, chapter of the NAACP, October 26, 1974.

TUCKER, K. D. *Needs Assessment Project,* Ocala: Central Florida Community Colleges Consortium, 1974–1975.

VACCARO, L. C. "The Manpower Development and Training Act and the Community College." *Junior College Journal,* 1963, *34,* 21–23.

VERMILYE, D. W. (Ed.) *The Expanded Campus: Current Issues in Higher Education.* San Francisco: Jossey-Bass, 1972.

VERMILYE, D. W. (Ed.) *Lifelong Learners—A New Clientele for Higher Education: Current Issues in Higher Education.* San Francisco: Jossey-Bass, 1974.

VERNER, C. "The Junior College as a Social Institution." In *Community Services in the Community Junior Colleges: Proceedings of the Annual Florida Junior College Conference.* Tallahassee: Florida State Department of Education, 1960.

WARREN, R. L. *Studying Your Community.* New York: Free Press, 1965.

WAGGONER, A. C. "Venture into Continuing Education." *Junior College Journal,* 1960, *30,* 44–49.

WEBB, K., and HATRY, H. P. *Obtaining Citizen Feedback: The Application of Citizen Surveys to Local Government.* Washington, D.C.: The Urban Institute, 1973.

WILLIAMS, G. S. "Developing Creative Leadership in Community Services." *Adult Leadership,* 1970, *36,* 51–52.

WISE, S. R., WYGAL, B. R., and TERRELL, C. R. "Service for an Urban Community." In Cohen, A. M., and Brawer, F. (Eds.), *Reaching Out Through Community Services.* San Francisco: Jossey-Bass, 1976.

WYGAL, B. R. *Community Needs—How Do We Identify Them?* Jacksonville: Florida Junior College, 1974.

WYGAL, B. R. "The Community College Connection: Community-Based Education." In C. R. Schenkman (Ed.), *A Policy Primer for Community-Based Community Colleges: Report of the 1974 Assembly of the American Association of Community and Junior Colleges.* Washington, D.C.: American Association of Community and Junior Colleges, 1975a.

WYGAL, B. R. "Will the Economy Crunch the Community-Based Movement?" *Community and Junior College Journal,* 1975b, *46*(3), 12–13.

YARRINGTON, R. (Ed.) *Educational Opportunity for All: An Agenda for National Action.* Washington, D.C.: American Association of Community and Junior Colleges, 1973.

YARRINGTON, R. (Ed.) *Educational Opportunity for All: New Staff for New Students.* Washington, D.C.: American Association of Community and Junior Colleges, 1974a.

YARRINGTON, R. "An Interview with Ervin Harlacher: What Does It Mean To Be Community-Based?" *Community and Junior College Journal,* 1974b, *45*(1), 13–15.

YARRINGTON, R. "Assessing the Community Base." *Community and Junior College Journal,* 1975, *46*(3), 7.

ZIEGERELL, J. J. "Community College in Search of an Identity." *Journal of Higher Education,* 1970, *41,* 701–712.

Index